TEENS ON THE EDGE...

TROUBLED TEENS SPEAK OUT
plus AUTHOR COMMENTARY

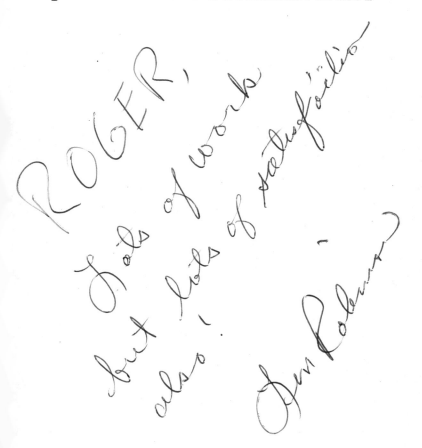

TEENS ON THE EDGE...

TROUBLED TEENS SPEAK OUT plus AUTHOR COMMENTARY

By

Len Robinson, M.A.
(Educator/Former School Principal)

Copyright © 2000 by Leonard Robinson, M.A.

All rights reserved.
No part of this book may be reproduced, stored in a retrieval system, or transmitted by any means, electronic, mechanical, photocopying, recording, or otherwise, without written permission from the author.

ISBN: 1-58721-395-8

1stBooks - rev. 6/14/00

ABOUT THE BOOK

Juvenile crime in America today is a threat to every one of us. It is the most discussed, feared, and blatantly misunderstood phenomenon confronting communities throughout the U.S.A.

Who listens to our troubled youth in America today? In their attitudes and often anti-social behaviors, today's young people cry out for help, desperate for someone to listen to them.

This book is powerfully focused on listening to the previously silent voices of teens in detention. Incarcerated teenagers (17 and 18 years of age, female and male, all races and ethnic backgrounds) face a critical juncture in their frenetic journey through life.

This is their story in their own words. Each story is unique yet alarmingly the same. Almost with One Voice these troubled teens reveal their stories of abuse, neglect and abandonment, struggling to find their place in the harsh world in which they find themselves.

These autobiographies represent not so much their failures as ours: parents, educators, communities, social institutions. All have failed to recognize the desperate cries for help from these youths, which are often manifested in various and disturbing disguises.

These essays are by teens who are studying for the GED [Graduate Equivalent Degree]. The author, their instructor, invited them to tell their story in their own faltering, often brutally blunt words.

To read these thirty-five+ raw, blunt essays is to bear witness to and participate in their troubled world of abuse, drugs, rampant sex, and violence. The author's commentary provides both background and illuminating insight into the core problem: theirs and society's.

The aim of the book is to awaken the profound need for societal involvement in these troubled teens so that we can begin to focus more profoundly on how to help them and eradicate or at least lessen the alarming problem of juvenile crime in America.

TEENS ON THE EDGE offers a profound and intimate examination of the core factors involved in juvenile crime and violence. American psychological and financial survival are at stake in resolving this problem. Our prisons are full of offenders who were themselves victims of severe childhood trauma or torture. While most children who endure abuse or neglect mature into law-abiding adults, the ones who do not become the menace so feared by the community, sapping it of billions of dollars in the process.

Many current books focus on various perspectives of dysfunctional families, troubled teens, child abuse, and youth violence and crime in America. This book complements them all, but is unique in combining all of the above phenomena into one powerful book.

No academic study or professional analyses have the same profound impact as listening to the troubled youths themselves!

ABOUT THE AUTHOR

Leonard Robinson, a licensed teacher and school administrator in Nevada, has had over thirty years of direct involvement with education, acquiring a vast knowledge of the subject of this book. For over fifteen years he worked directly with the Nevada court system serving as both school principal and teacher for Clark County. Recipient of the Distinguished Service Award from the Clark County School District, Robinson also received a statewide Nevada Proclamation declaring October 23, 1987, <u>Leonard Robinson Day</u> from Governor Richard Bryan who presently serves as United States Senator. He has letters of commendation from the Director of Juvenile Court Services and the Superintendent of Schools, Clark County, Nevada. The State Parent/Teacher Association (PTA) awarded him a lifetime membership in recognition of his outstanding contributions to the welfare of children and youth in Nevada. Gene Feher, Executive Director of the National Juvenile Detention Association (NJDA) from 1981 to 1985 and presently a Trainer and Consultant for them writes in the book's preface, "He is demanding, energetic, and an outspoken advocate for necessary diversification and change!"

TABLE OF CONTENTS

Preface: Gene Feher, M.A. xi
Introduction by Author xiii

Chapters:

1. ABANDONED CHILDREN: Dysfunctional Beginnings 1

2. GANG INVOLVEMENT: A Need To Belong 19

3. PATTERNS REPEATED: Facing Tough Odds 37

4. DRUG REHABILITATON: Use On Upward Ascendance .. 53

5. PROSTITUTION: Only Recourse For Troubled Females 75

6. ABUSE NEGLECT: Desperate Cries For Help 99

7. GANGSTER PROSE & POETRY: Creative Endeavors 121

8. THE MISSION: Solutions 137

Appendix: Awards and Letters of Commendation 157

PREFACE
by Gene Feher, M.A.

I've know Leonard Robinson for well over twenty years-- from when he and I worked together at juvenile detention and later at Spring Mountain Youth Camp in Clark County, Nevada. Both facilities deal with students experiencing severe social problems which eventually manifest themselves in criminal behavior. Len started in the late seventies as principal at the Youth Camp and eventually was assigned supervision of all the educational facilities connected with court schools, including Child Haven for abused and neglected children. After retiring briefly he returned to juvenile detention to teach the older--17 and 18 years--students GED through the Adult Education Program.

In this book, he has recorded the minutiae of the lives of these children in a way that no other author has ever done. These personal essays capture a behind-the-scenes look at the dark, secret and dangerous life of the juvenile who is involved in this world. This book will eminently benefit the adult community, allowing them to focus on and gain an understanding of the dilemmas faced by the professionals in the field. After the fog of drugs and alcohol lifts these kids describe their lives from a stark, desperate perspective.

Len worked with the juvenile courts for well over fifteen years as a principal and teacher, utilizing all the experience he had garnered while working in the "regular" schools in those same capacities. With each student he had one simple goal: to educate and prepare that person for the next challenge. His work with incarcerated and abused children has been a special challenge. These children are a maze of contradictions and paradoxes, as capable of treachery as loyalty; children of exceptional charm and incredible gaucheries--children of many parts.

He learned his craft well. His educational experiences include assignments at many grade levels within the curriculum including a wide array of subject areas. His decision to accept the principalship with the court schools came at a time when he was very comfortable at Dearing Elementary School--this however was the challenge he sought. Preceeding this was a seven year stint as sixth grade center principal during the integration of the public schools in this Nevada community.

He has always been active in the community and is a very familiar figure on the political scene. His work as a lobbyist for the teachers and the school administrators brought him many accolades including an honorary lifetime membership in the state Parent/Teacher Association.

Throughout his career he has invited creative, innovative teachers to join him in providing an energetic yet warm, non-intimidating learning opportunity for these children. He is demanding, energetic, and an outspoken advocate for necessary diversification and change!

—Gene Feher, M.A.
Assistant Director, Detention
Clark County, Nevada

BIOGRAPHICAL NOTE

Gene served as the Executive Director of the National Juvenile Detention Association from 1981 to 1985. He presently is a trainer and consultant for the National Council of Juvenile and Family Court Judges, the American Correctional Association, and the National Juvenile Detention Association. In addition he is an auditor and consultant for the Commission on Accreditation for Corrections, and criminal justice instructor for Clark County Community College of Nevada. The author of TEACHING PARENTS, "Common Sense", he worked closely with the Sunrise Rotary of Boulder City, Nevada to develop this book providing "insight to helping your children deal with real life challenges they may face on a daily basis".*

---
*Boulder City Sunrise Rotary, Publishers - 1995

INTRODUCTION

This book--a collection of essays and author commentary--can be read from several perspectives. The essays themselves are written by incarcerated teenagers (17 years old--minimum age for GED training--to 18 years) who face a critical juncture in their journey through life. In 1787 Thomas Jefferson wrote in a letter to James Madison this obiter dictum, "Educate and inform the whole mass of people. Enable them to see that it is to their interest to preserve peace and order...They are the only sure reliance for the preservation of our liberty."* After thirty years in public education, fifteen years as a teacher/administrator of juvenile court schools, it is my conviction we must redouble our efforts to educate and inform if we are to heal a country plagued by gangs who can't find a way to coexist and are doggedly determined to codestruct.

Each one of their stories is both unique and alarmingly the same. They reveal experiences that most of us cannot imagine or would wish upon anyone we know. These stories of abuse, neglect, abandonment,* and more, reveal a harsh world: unfiltered and raw; a life with diffuse and often distorted perspectives of the familiar, the new, and the unknown. Reading these essays is to bear witness to and participate in the lives of these youngsters, lives they have been forced to live convulsively, compulsively, and beyond reason or meaning. Briefly, their lives may become our lives, as we are confronted with their unhealthy and often self-negating and self-destructive perceptions of how life is. These stories may force us to search deeply into the meaning of our own lives and those of our children; and we may feel compelled to "complete" their stories in our own mind. Each story has something meaningful to convey to us, as their childish, immature, desperate, and

---

* _____ Daniel B. Baker, <u>Power Quotes</u>, Visible Ink Press, 1992

unfiltered voices call out to us for a moment--and then disappear, becoming as lost as these youths appear to be.

These stories represent not so much failed children as they do failed parents, failed communities, failed social institutions, and failures to recognize desperate cries for help. For many teenagers, their painful cries began as young as four or five years of age, when their anti-social behavior first began to manifest itself. These pleas were often met with a brusque, knee-jerk reaction that said: "Come back when you are older and become a real threat to our well being; then we will deal with you." Sadly, this is the point at which the youngsters in the book find themselves.

These teenage girls and boys are now studying for the GED (Graduate Equivalent Degree). As they struggle with the demands of the classroom, their thoughts wander to life on "the streets" and to the bizarre yet enticing workings of that dark underbelly of society. This book vividly explores the full spectrum of the human drama as it manifests in the chilling and mysterious world of juvenile crime.

The President's Council of Economic Advisers' newly released statistics indicate the nation is making gains regarding the wellbeing of our youth. Less than 2 percent of children go hungry in a year, children who live in poverty are visiting doctors more often, and the number of children living in crowded housing dropped from 9 percent in 1978 to 6 percent in 1997. Yet these gains have not prevented our communities from experiencing a social breakdown in many critical areas. Children are progressively exposed to readily available and easily accessed drugs, violence is more prevalent, more youth are being incarcerated, and increasing numbers will become parents before they complete school. "Improving the odds for children in low-income communities will require many things including greater access to supports that all families need to raise kids successfully-employment opportunities for parents, quality health care, formal and informal networks of adults...vibrant religious institutions, organized recreation, and safe streets...But of all the community institutions that help children become capable adults, perhaps none is more important than school"

(The Annie E. Casey Foundation, <u>Kids Count Data Book</u>, 1997).

Moreover, it is becoming increasingly clear that children are desperately dependent on their parents for guidance, and perhaps most importantly expectations. If parents set low standards for their children it is extremely difficult to offset the ill effects of this. Robert J. Samuelson (<u>Newsweek</u>, 2-23-98) writes that the investments "that really count for children come from parents: love and security, discipline and instruction, a sense of worth. Being rich is no guarantee that parents will provide these; being poor is no indicator that they won't. But large federal programs, whatever their benefits, can't undo parental failure. Nor can they offset the ill effects of family breakdown. To think otherwise sanctions the behaviors that put children at risk."

We must be careful when we weigh the statistics and rhetoric concerning these children that we do not become too pessimistic about the prospects for some and avoid unwarranted complacency about others. It is a complicated yet captivating perplexity quacunque via data (whichever way you take it).

Chapter One

ABANDONED CHILDREN
Dysfunctional Beginnings

Imagine this scene from a troublesome night in the life of a typical "gangster" (as they call themselves) who's involved in the different facets of a life of crime on the mean streets of any U.S.A. city:

"You live in an abandoned apartment where a few of your "homies" (trusted friends) are enjoying smack (heroin) as they discuss the omnipotent need for even more smack and other necessities, such as money. After serving eight months in the state juvenile detention center, you're determined to minimize your risks, because freedom tastes "real good" right now. But you have one major worry; when you turn eighteen shortly, you'll be charged as an adult on your next arrest. Adulthood opens up a whole series of new legal problems which you want to delay as much as possible!

"Stealing, robbing, selling drugs, car theft, and similar illegal activities, have been your primary source of money for years. You have spent a large portion of your young life locked up in juvenile institutions due to multiple arrests on virtually any charge that could be imposed. You've spent little or no time in school or working at a job to attain the skills needed in the workplace."

The above scenario is a sketch of the typical disadvantaged teen who has had negative encounters with the law. The common profile is that virtually all of them are from broken homes or homes so dysfunctional that they mirror the worst aspects of family life, or any semblance of it. Often these dysfunctional teens are shifted from place to place, grounded in instability, and exposed to drugs at a vulnerable age (preteens). Either they themselves are the victims of violence or have witnessed violence being inflicted upon a parent, sibling, or other intimate family member. For most, it is all they know of life, and violence becomes the apparent "norm" for them.

As youngsters they have had very little material or emotional security beyond bare essentials, and some even deficient in those. They have been shifted from person to person with no one genuinely caring or being legitimately involved to offer any nurturing or support. Finally, most of these youth become involved in gangs. Many of the females with a pimp. All desperately searching for protection and solidity, and a sense of belonging which has been denied them.

Surprisingly, despite these negative odds against them, most have managed to do fairly well in school until fifth or sixth grade. Then the sheer realities of life overwhelmed them and they sought alternatives. Most of these teens can actually pinpoint the time when their activities caused their descent into self-destructive behavior, eventually escalating into illegal activities.

Drugs are the common enemy and the grease which makes this whole sub-culture function. Drugs provide two crucial components of their life: a means of escape and a way to finance their negative lifestyle. Gangs, guns, drugs, stealing, robbing, and prostitution comprise their essential existence. On the outside fringe of all this is their other activity of choice: making babies.

Before further commentary, it is important that we read the essays and examine the experiences of the students. Basically these essays are published in their original text. The phraseology, grammatical errors, and spelling remain intact, except where basic clarity dictated minor corrections.

The editing primarily clarified passages which were obscure, rambling, or totally unstructured. The author consulted with the writers of the essays to insure that their intent and meaning remained intact after we made spelling and grammatical changes. The names have been changed to protect their identity.

JANE'S STORY

Seventeen-year-old-Jane was arrested in a tavern for

soliciting for prostitution. In the classroom setting, you'd never connect her to such a scene. A small, delicate-looking black girl, she had a strong aversion to looking directly at you when conversing. Many of her mannerisms are indicative of someone closer to thirteen years of age.

Quiet and withdrawn at first, she opened up as she became comfortable with me and the other students. The school materials for GED prep are geared to the student's educational attainment level, and she quickly became comfortable in this setting, especially when she received attention. She wanted lots of individual assistance and frequently came to my desk for help as well as conversation which she needed emotionally.

During one of our talks she called herself a "ho", a term I found unfamiliar. I had heard the word before in snatches of conversation, but the meaning never really registered. On her sheet of criminal charges it became obvious she used "ho" to mean "whore."

I saw absolutely no correlation between this little, bashful, rather plain-looking girl and the stereotypical prostitute. Gentle and trusting, it seemed impossible to imagine the scene during her arrest.

Read her short dissertation carefully. It is apparent she had absolutely no chance to overcome the obstacles continuously thrown in her path. CHARGES:[*] solicitation for prostitution, obstructing a police officer, violating curfew, and resisting arrest

JANE: ESSAY #1

"I was born in Maine, moved West and lived in a house when I was tiny, probably about one. My mother got a job but it did not last very long and she got laid off. We had to move out of the house and we was on the street homeless. The only home I know about was the streets we stayed on. We stayed on the

---

[*] Throughout this book the word 'CHARGES' will refer to the offenses filed during booking into juvenile detention.

streets until I was eight years old and then I was taken to a group home.

"When I was twelve-years-old I just couldn't stand that group home and I ran away and moved in with a friend. That was when I began to run the street. I started to be a Ho (prostitute). That was the only thing that I know how to do. My mom did not tell me nothing else.

"Finally I was caught and had to go back to another group home. It was just like the last one and they decided they couldn't handle me and sent me to my father's home. Well, he made me to have sex with him and I couldn't stand that so I ran away again. Since I didn't know what else to do I became a Ho again and have been a Ho since then.

"Here is my whole life. I have been a Ho since I was twelve years old. I have been shot and stabbed since I been a Ho. I've been shot at more than once. I have had a pimp since I was twelve years old.

"I like my new life now. I did not like it at one time. One time I tried to kill myself. But I don't think like that no more. I'm a Ho still and I have a pimp still. Thank you. Bye. It is how I live my life."

COMMENTARY

The stark simplicity and emotionless tone of this essay reveal one of the gut-wrenching stories which are far too typical of the appalling existence endured by the neglected and abused children. What metamorphosis did this child endure to reach the point where she surrenders without a murmur to the existence inflicted upon her? The tone of hopeless resignation is apparent in her conclusion, "It is how I live my life."

LOLA'S STORY

This next person was very closed, barely able to communicate with anyone beyond one or two words. She had a white father, Hispanic mother, and had spent most of her life being passed back and forth between her parents and her maternal grandmother. Her physical unattractiveness had more to do with her constant scowl and blank stare than with her actual physical features.

Devoid of classroom skills, she could not, or would not, attempt the most basic assignment. Most youngsters who are impoverished in the classroom either want to draw, listen to music on headphones, or passively thumb through magazines. Lola wanted nothing to do with anything remotely connected to education. She seemed content to sit through the two hour class scowling at me or any classmate who came too close to her desk or committed any perceived aggression toward her.

Sometimes these teens refuse to divulge any pertinent details about their life. Encouraged to write on any subject she chose, Lola would give only an abbreviated glimpse of her life. Perhaps, in retrospect, she actually spoke volumes in her three sentence autobiography. To attempt an understanding of Lola we are forced to extrapolate some meaning from what little she wrote and try to discern what her cursory message might actually mean. CHARGES: obstructing a police officer, false information, violating curfew, possession of controlled substance, possession with intent to sell

LOLA: ESSAY #2

"In my life I have a man. His name is Roberto. He love me and I have his baby name Roberta."

COMMENTARY

In a nutshell this reveals what is most important in her life. Her man, her baby, and that someone loves her. This is her whole world. It is highly doubtful that her man could support her, and Lola had only the very slightest hope of passing the GED test and eventually securing any meaningful employment. She especially exemplifies the need to open vocational avenues to young people. With meaningful guidance and direction perhaps she could be guided to some vocation. If not, she will have to grasp the only life she knows and the cycle begins anew:

further incarceration, increased constrictions on that overburdened system, and her baby becoming involved in the "mix" (their word for the criminal underbelly of society).

The male population manifests a slightly different set of circumstances that confront these teens. Most seem compelled to commit crimes that will drastically alter their lives as they scramble to stay in sync with the violence that surrounds them.

JAMES'S STORY

James, 17, is not typical of the average young man incarcerated at juvenile detention. His basic intelligence, educational attainment, and demeanor all belie his current status. If not for the orange jumpsuit worn by all detainees he would look like any young "preppie" involved in preparatory studies for college.

His movie-star looks closely resemble the late James Dean with his blonde-brownish hair and chiseled features. His body is fully sculpted with well-developed muscles in his arms and legs, creating an impressive image. On the outdoor basketball court he is distinctly in charge as the point guard, moving players around and feeding the open man.

In the classroom he is the image of a serious student intent on absorbing as much as he can in two hours. We disagreed only once, a strange experience. James objected to a mapping assignment. He questioned the need to do it, questioned the availability of appropriate research materials, and questioned my motives in assigning it.

During this disagreement, he leaned across the desk; his eyes narrowed, his knuckles turned white as they clenched the sides of the desk, and his voice became strained, resembling a croak. I hadn't sensed the seriousness of his distress and knew at that point he needed to be removed from class to regain his composure.

This was before the court had assigned their staff to be present in the classrooms, and I had to ease him out of the room without a major confrontation. I slowly rolled my chair back and stood up. He came around the desk and stood within six inches of my face, glowering and making his strange croaking sound. Walking very slowly and deliberately to the door, I motioned to a caseworker outside the room.

The caseworker stood slightly wedged between the two of us. When he questioned what had occurred, James's croaking became a loud hum, and I sensed he was really losing it. As I backed away, he tried to lunge at me. Quickly, the caseworker adeptly clutched both his arms behind his back and, with the help of another staff, secured his arms and legs.

After a twenty-four hour lockdown James returned to the classroom, apparently unaffected by our confrontation. He requested a change allowing him to do a research paper on early America. Although his booking sheet listed him as Caucasian, he often alluded to being part Indian. He had a strong interest in anything dealing with Native Americans. CHARGES: possession dangerous weapon, under the influence controlled substance, possession of firearm, possession of controlled substance w/intent to sell

JAMES: ESSAY #3

"I was born and raised to the age of seven in a nice little trailer park with my brothers and sisters. During this period of time my mother and father were constantly fighting and my father finally took off.

"My mother couldn't handle everything and said she would have to send me to live with my grandma and grandfather. She had already sent my brothers out there and when I arrived they said we were living in the biggest gang pit around there. Our gang was called 'Shires' because we lived around Wilshire Park Avenue

"All of the brothers were in this gang, using drugs and never attending school. It got so bad that they sent me back here when I was thirteen. Nothing changed. All I did was fight at school, rob houses, shoot at people, etc.

"When I got in to high school I was so out of control it was unbelievable. I sold and used drugs, guns, and anything else I could market. This got me kicked out of every high school I attended.

"During my high school years I was arrested for attempted murder, auto burglary, battery with a deadly weapon, battery with bodily harm, burglary, possession with intent to sell and many runaways. My parents got remarried when I was thirteen and really didn't want me underfoot. I hated being there and ran whenever it got too bad.

"When I was sixteen I fell in love with my fiance, Lois, and we had a son together. Her parents were dead from a drug overdose so they couldn't interfere, but my parents did not approve and were a real pain.

"I worked two jobs as long as I could to keep a roof over our heads and food on the table, but after our son was born complications set in. Lois had to have a C-section and was flat on her back for a month. I had to work and take care of Lois and our son. So...I sold drugs to get the money I needed. Fast food wouldn't cut it and that is why I'm here."

COMMENTARY

It would be interesting to hear James's rational for being "under the influence" when arrested. Being as bright as he is, he logically knew he was conspicuously enhancing his probability of being arrested. Fast food may not 'cut it' but it absolutely provided a better choice than drugs.

With his intelligence and drive he'll no doubt pass the GED test. What he does with the degree is the question. He could easily handle community college work and would also do well in a variety of vocational training slots. His probation officer committed to monitoring his case closely and felt that with counseling James on anger control there existed the distinct possibility he would respond positively when released.

James typifies, through his family profile, many of the students in juvenile detention. He has one son and will undoubtedly continue to have children although his ability to properly nurture and raise a child is questionable. James was essentially abandoned at age seven. Would he consider doing the same to his own child? What would happen if his violent temper flared while he cared for his son?

Many states are now placing teenage parenting especially under stern scrutiny. Too many disasters have occurred when a child is left with an inappropriate parent, resulting in another grim story of abuse. Faced with the reality of a record number of children being killed because of abuse and neglect, states such as Oregon want to end parental rights within one year if the parent is deemed inappropriate. In 1996, Oregon drafted Senate Bill 689 which required the State Office for Services to Children to make two plans; one to return the child home and another to provide alternative, permanent housing at the end of a one year period.

Essentially states such as Oregon are saying children cannot be left in limbo. During the fall 1996 session of the State legislature Timothy Travis, a Portland attorney, said that SB-689 would "get tough on the child-welfare agency; it gets tough on parents and on judges" (The Oregonian, 3-27-97). He worked with a coalition of lawyers, doctors, judges, and children's advocates to draft it.

This basic attitude toward abuse and neglect of children is being echoed throughout the United States.

These changes, while admirable, carry a price tag that each state must zealously pledge to meet if they are to be effective. They are: 1] Increase the number of caseworkers significantly. 2] Increase financing to the state agency handling services to children. 3] Most importantly, exercise diligence and imagination in securing permanent homes for these children. This final process will require more funding to implement but may be more cost effective in the long run. Bouncing a child from foster home to foster home is at present the only option; for the child almost as stressful. In Oregon, hiring 160 caseworkers to execute this plan would increase the State Office for Services to Children and Family budget by 36 percent. The total budget including federal funds would increase to $450 million dollars. This is a huge increase in funding but, like Oregon, something each state must be determined to implement.

What contributes most significantly to the tidal wave of

neglect and abuse? The increasing phenomenon of children who have, and attempt to raise children. As this phenomenon invades society it may well become the nation's leading domestic crisis.

The next two essays are very different, yet very similar. Both written by young men who have embarked on fatherhood with a vengeance. Their stories are disturbing in their tone and implication.

TYRONE'S STORY

A seventeen year old black youth, Tyrone lived on the borderline, avoiding involvement in any major criminal activity or imprisonment. But this is changing as his responsibilities increase. He is forced to take more chances as he feels the financial pressure of additional family obligations.

Outwardly he's not particularly motivated, yet he accomplishes a lot in class and is fairly successful with material that sparks his interest. A frail young man, he looks in his early teens, until you look more closely at his face! He has pockmarks from a childhood disease, and the wrinkles around his eyes clearly hint at suffering he endured. His entire body reflects his intensity when he is consumed with learning a new math concept or in applying that concept to one of the questions likely to be on the test.

Tyrone is difficult to talk to, many of his expressions are foreign to me as well as to most of his friends in the cottage. They laughed at how he described things. When I sat with Tyrone to edit his essay, he demanded leaving some things intact. His essay has descriptions that raise questions about his real meaning. For example: He described his babies and their mother as 'just bitches, stupid!' Tyrone assured me these were meant as compliments where he came from. When I asked where, he was vague, he didn't want anyone 'meddlin' with his past.

Tyrone, like his peers here, felt he could successfully function while consuming drugs, insisting drugs were not a major part of his life; they were used as a calming influence "when he felt a little nervous." Charges: burglary, possession of stolen property, obstruction of police officer, under influence controlled substance

TYRONE: ESSAY #4

"In mid-December at a very early hour of the morning I was pulled over by a policeman for no reason. He searched the car and took me to juvenile detention and booked me. I had been placed in the holding area over night before. Not this time! They just put me over here in long term. I don't like it! I have five kids of my own; three boys, two boys twins and one lil one, and two girls. Including the babies' mother, they all like crazy, not about me, they just bitches, stupid!

"But out of all of them I only love one of them. Well, I love all of them but the craziest one I love the most. I don't know what she's done to me but I can't wait to get out and just hold her. My lil girl in my arms.

"I try to tell the younger kids in the cottages that this is not the place to be but they do not listen. They're hardheaded I guess. They must like it here, but I don't! I want to be with my own kids and talk to them and tell them that this is not the place to go, not the place to be, nothing like that.

"I have to tell you. My mom and dad died in front of my eyes when I was seven. The guys who killed them I wish would have killed me too. Instead they let me live. Why they do that?

"I try not to let stuff get to me but it is hard being locked up with no mom or dad, no one to talk to. I have no one to turn to but my girl, my lady. That is why I want to get out of here and do good and not come back!

"That is all I want the judge to do. Just give me one more chance. I sit in my room and sometimes cry because it hurts me to remember what I have been through and what I am going through right now. I pray that someone hears me screaming for help before it's too late. Please. Someone help me. Please."

COMMENTARY

A chilling summation of a life that began with a scenario too hideous and ghastly for most of us to fully envision and grasp. What is he really asking when he refers to the 'guys who killed them,' adding, 'They let me live. Why they do that?'

My gut instinct says he is suicidal. Staff watched him closely, never leaving him even for brief periods. What would become of his family if he killed himself? More significantly, what guidance will Tyrone exert over his family? Tyrone and his 'girl' are both abandoned children who flit on the threshold of endangering their own children.

Parenthood is often discussed in the cottages as bragging ritual with the boys, with heavy macho overtones. A male child is clearly the first choice, but they are proud of all their babies and will father more in the future. As a group they exhibited no inkling of the economic and social obligations inherent in parenthood.

HERMAN'S STORY

Herman started his "mission" to beget a family earlier than most. His baby face and general demeanor of an immature teenager rebelling against life belies his being the father of several children.

His mother and father, white, middle class, with successful careers, have little time for each other or their child. Growing up, Herman hardly saw either parent, though he lived in their house for over fifteen years. He and his girlfriend had their first child at age fourteen. Herman was very vague about where she lived and what arrangements they had for taking care of their offspring.

What little information he gave of his family sounded strange and quite beyond the fringe of normal lifestyles. His father was either on the road, home playing tennis and golf, or out with his 'bitch,' while his mother was simply not around, particularly on weekends.

Herman has a long history of drug use beginning with marijuana in seventh grade. He admits the drug has been his nemesis in school and hindered him in his job search.

CHARGES: possession controlled substance, shoplifting, false information, obstruction of police officer

HERMAN: ESSAY #5

"I lived in a small town in Oklahoma until I was seven years old and moved to Seattle. I did all right in school and at home until I was thirteen and started seventh grade.

"I started hanging around the wrong crowd and fighting everybody for no reason. I made it through seventh grade smoking weed daily. I went to school until I reached eighth grade then it all changed. I started ditching school instead of just getting high at lunch. Me and my friends would ditch the whole day and get high at each others' house.

"Ninth grade I started to get serious, going to school every day and getting good grades. Then these two kids moved into my neighborhood and we started going to school to sell dope only, no classes. I finally got busted, expelled from the school district and sent to juvenile hall for twelve days. During that twelve days they charged me but said it wouldn't count unless I got another arrest. Then I would be going to court for distribution and whatever the new charge turned out to be.

"I got caught shoplifting two weeks later and went back to juvenile hall. They released me to my parents and said they would set a court date. My girl and I talked it over and decided that it was stupid to wait around for them to put me in jail so we split.

"We were doing great until they told me I had to have a Sheriff's card in order to work in this little town we settled in. I handed them my drivers license and ten minutes later they arrested me on the warrants from my home state. My home state was glad to get rid of me and dropped the charges after my lawyer contacted them.

"I was beginning to feel a little desperate because I have lots of obligations. When I was fourteen I got with my girl and we have had two kids since with a third one on the way. Her parents do not even acknowledge we exist and I can't really count on my parents that much. Both my mother and father said many times they wanted me out of their hair!

"All the contacts I made in this little town were with the wrong crowd once again. They all smoked a lot of weed, sold a lot of weed, and were watched constantly by the fuzz (police). They talked me into doing some crazy stuff and I got busted (arrested) for grand theft auto, avoiding and obstructing a police officer, assault, burglary, and possession of stolen property. My lawyer got me off with six months probation for all those charges and I was feeling pretty good.

"I knew the cops would be watching me because they didn't expect to see me on the streets so soon. I hardly started my probation before they had me up on phony auto burglary and obstruction charges. They didn't have enough evidence and had to drop those charges. My lawyer said they would try to get me on any kind of trumped up charges and warned me to stay clean.

"They eventually nailed me on a little old trespassing charge after I got that other mess cleared up and I willingly said fifteen hours of community service sounded fair. They tried to stiff (charge) me with assault and battery but that was dropped.

"I finished my fifteen hours of community service but they still put me on probation and assigned me to a thirty day program where I was monitored to see if I was going to make it. They monitored me so closely that I could barely move. I ended up getting arrested for burglary again, released through my attorney, and almost immediately arrested again and charged with burglary, breaking and entering, trespassing, petty larceny and assault and battery when I tried to escape.

"My lawyer kept getting my case continued hoping that when I turned eighteen the judge would dismiss the case. This might have worked but the next month I was caught shoplifting and when they searched me they found a joint (marijuana cigarette) and some roaches (smoked marijuana cigarette).

"The judge decided to put me in here until I turn eighteen next month. I feel like my parents will totally desert me when I turn eighteen but that is all right because all I want to do is get home to my kids and my girl."

COMMENTARY

Herman is not ready to deal with the adult prison system. He is a soft, almost effeminate young man who would be an easy target for predators who inhabit the prisons. With no job skills, a heavy financial burden supporting his ever enlarging family, and no parental help from either his or his girlfriend's parents, his future looks rather bleak.

Herman was not abandoned by his parents when they issued that last check to his lawyers when he turned eighteen. He was never a part of a warm caring family that is so necessary for children in their early formative years. Recent studies indicate a mother's touch may be the ingredient that is most necessary for a child's well-being later in life. Professor Robert M. Sapolsy of Stanford University writes that new research "must spur on work examining how early experience alters the trajectory of our own development" (Science, 9-12-97). The "mother's touch" is a prosaic void in the lives of youth incarcerated in juvenile detention.

Most of these children were substantially abandoned long before they reached eighteen. That is why they cling to one another like a life preserver believing there is no other alternative. They go through the motions of trying to be adultlike, playing house, having babies, and bringing home necessities. None of it works very well because they are simply not equipped for real adult life or the demands of having a family to support, care for, and nurture.

When youngsters are abandoned, physically or emotionally or both by their parents, they seek an alternative for their missing family. Desperate for a sense of belonging, they start their own family. "The percentage of all births to unmarried mothers has risen significantly, up from 5 percent in 1960 to 32 percent in 1995" (L. A. Times, 7-3-97). The article also concluded that in 1966, a similar 32 percent of the nations children lived with one parent, up significantly from 15 percent in 1970. Society must somehow intervene in this dangerous cycle if their offspring are afforded even a remote chance regarding normal childhood. We must recognize illegitimacy as the smoking gun in a frightening array of pathologies; crime, drug abuse, mental and physical illness, and welfare dependency.

Imagine the fate of the children born to Herman or Tyrone or any other teen mentioned here. How long before Tyrone or Herman are separated from their families either through incarceration or another type of abandonment? The bulk of support for their young families already is being discharged by society and that will increase as they become older. Is there a way of healing these dysfunctional families? The Aid to Families with Dependent Children (AFDC) accounts for only one percent of all federal expenditures and has been declining, rather than increasing, in proportion to other spending. We have heard an incredible amount of rhetoric on the subject but there is a huge gap between the talk and governmental commitment.

Obviously, these two boys are ill-equipped to fulfill the role of parent. They have no <u>legal</u> means of financially supporting their families. Given their personal problems with substance abuse, the violent lives they lead, and their tendency to become involved in gang activity there is little time in their lives for parenting; a task they are ill-equipped to carry out.

The Kappan Special Report points out that "more than 20 percent of American children live in poverty, an increase of more than one-third since 1970. The immediate costs of investment in the future pale beside the long-run costs of failing to invest. The Children at Risk Project, currently providing intensive interventions for selected poor children in six cities, costs $4,000 per child, per year. On the other hand, it costs more than $20,000 a year to keep a youth in prison. According to Nobel Laureate economist Robert Solow, the consequences of child poverty costs America $36 billion a year" (<u>Phi Delta Kappan</u>, March 1995).

The Census Bureau reports that in 1995, "Children raised in single-parent homes do not fare as well economically as children with both parents at home, but children of divorced parents are better off financially than children of a parent who was never married. Unemployment among never-married mothers was nearly twice as high as that of divorced mothers who are raising their children. Fifty-nine percent of never-married mothers were unemployed while twenty-nine percent of divorced mothers were without a job" (<u>Las Vegas Review Journal/Sun</u>, 2-15-98). This economic disadvantage is likely to vanish in the event of marriage or remarriage. I never came across one incarcerated parent (student) in detention who was married or even considered it an important item for discussion.

In the same article quoted above the Princeton University researchers in Family Planning Perspectives, a journal from the Alan Guttmacher Institute, reported that teenagers under fifteen have a very high risk-ratio in childbearing resulting in a host of problems. The report shows a "relationship between a mother's age and a baby's low birth weight, infant mortality and hospitalization costs. Of more than 200,000 births, more black females were likely to give birth as teenagers...while the costs of babies born to white mothers younger than fifteen" are among the highest of all the groups studied. The younger the mother, the worse the birth outcome. "Age isn't the only thing that is going on, it is education and social class, and age often masks that," said Deanna Pagnini, assistant professor of sociology and public affairs at Princeton (Ibid.).

The lack of family structure and education, joblessness, and instability brings on poverty, unemployment, and delinquency. We must break the cycle. "Children are the living message we send to a time we will not see" (Anonymous).

Chapter 2

GANG INVOLVEMENT
A Need To Belong

Could any of you imagine your own son or daughter involved in a violent gang? Families in middle-class neighborhoods feel they have successfully avoided gang exposure for their own children. Their neighborhoods are free of that plague. This false sense of security has lured many parents into a state of somnolence while their children pursue unsavory activities.

When parents enter the juvenile detention Center to identify their child and discover there is gang-involvement their first reaction is denial, gradually followed by total shock. After I've talked to parents, they finally see, in hindsight, warning signs which they chose to ignore. The signs? Failing school courses, school disciplinary problems, and chaotic or unstable personal and social life. These signs were ignored or attributed to other causal factors, such as low self esteem, lack of basic skills, uncaring teachers, ineffective school discipline, growing pains, along with others.

The stereotypes of typical gang members are that they are racial and ethnic minorities who come from poor families, and live in single-parent households. Statistics did reveal that these impoverished youngsters have a higher propensity for gang involvement. However, no economic level of society is exempt. Poor white neighborhoods are as gang infested as comparable neighborhoods containing largely minority residents. The Clark County School District (CCSD) Police Department in Nevada states that "kids in gangs come from all economic backgrounds." No U.S.A. neighborhood today is totally exempt from the impact of gangs.

The CCSD Police Department Gang Advisory pamphlet reads: "There are white kids in predominantly black, Hispanic, and Asian gangs. There are even up and coming white gangs. It was always believed that the children in gangs came from low-income families and had low self-esteem; which is not true." The pamphlet emphasizes the perception that only minorities are gang involved is to look at the problem with blinders.

Police and juvenile caseworkers describe three distinct levels of gang involvement: hardcore, associate, and 'wannabe,' the latter are kids on the fringe of the gang movement who are highly vulnerable to this exposure. Anyone affiliated on any of the three levels authorities consider "potentially dangerous."

Hardcore gang members are easily identified: they are very actively involved, have an extensive history of gang involvement, and are self-proclaimed, gang participants. Those known as associates, have not been "jumped" into a gang (had the initiation ritual), but hang with (affiliates) and know gangsters (AKA gang members).

Lewis Yablonsky's book Gangsters: 50 years of Madness, Drugs, and Death on the Streets of America* focuses on today's violent gangs. He writes: (a gang) "is not merely a group of juvenile delinquents. We're not talking about the Bowery Boys with baggy pants. This is a much more lethal organization." He describes how these gangs 'graduated' from street fights to murder.

The essays in this chapter describe childhood experiences, arising from hardcore association with gangs. The students are all gang members with an extensive history of gang involvement. Their terminology is liberally sprinkled with terms used almost exclusively in the gang lingo. With the widespread media coverage, most will be easily understood.*

BACKGROUND ON GANGS

To be 'jumped' into a gang a child has to pass their initiation ritual, a test of courage where the recruit fight off other gang members for a specified period of time. Though lasting one or

---

* New York University Press, 1997

two minutes, it is extremely physical and the recruit usually emerges bloodied with his elan severely tested. The anointed ones can become gang members through a 'court-in.' This is where he (or she) is allowed to enlist by invitation of an O.G. (Original Gangster). An O.G. is a gang member who has the name, rank, and honor acquired only by the upper echelon.

Students often talk about their 'hood', which is their neighborhood as defined by the tagging (gang writing) gangs do to mark off their territory. Taggers (so-called artisans who display their work on walls, etc.) are entirely different and will be described in the last chapter of this book.

Why would a youngster join a gang? Police, educators, and social workers agree that one of the most compelling reasons is 'peer fear.' For a variety of reasons these teens feel the need for back-up (reinforcement) before, during, and after school. Many of them live in violent areas and have no one to talk with about their fears. Parents or guardians are either not available themselves or feel helpless when they're confronted with these fears.

Many diverse factors are at work within a gang. The gang is a microcosm, the world in miniature, which offers what most of these children consider basic necessities: an extended family of brothers and sisters, protection, sustenance. Factored into this are drugs, a variety of illegal activities, violence, sexual relationships, and a fairly complicated set of redesigned beliefs which replace traditional family values.

TONYA'S STORY

Tonya, is a beautiful, articulate, Hispanic girl nearing her eighteenth birthday. Her big brown eyes are very expressive, and you can read her moods by her eyes. Her naturally black hair has patches of enhanced blonde throughout. She has the body and look of a young beauty in the sweatsuit which she wears to school. However, playing outdoor volleyball in shorts and t-shirt, she projects a totally different image--virtually all of her exposed skin is covered with assorted tattoos.

In and out of gangs for much of her seventeen years, she

recognizes the need to completely re-evaluate her entire life. She will need a tremendous amount of support and guidance if she is to avoid the pitfalls which have caused her to be incarcerated.

As I sat at my desk one afternoon talking with her cousin (a term used for both a close friend and blood relative), Tonya came up and asked if she could interrupt. Her cousin generously offered her the seat, and Tonya proceeded to talk very quickly and in rather hushed tones. She had expected placement in Independent Living, which is a closely supervised setup which still gives them some autonomy. Instead she'd been consigned to a lock-up facility in a rural location.

The boys had not yet arrived for class and Tonya talked freely and openly about her dilemma. Suddenly, she stared directly into my eyes and pleaded "marry me, adopt me, take me as a foster child, anything, but please don't let them take me there!" I've been shocked by many things students have said over the years but this desperation stunned me. She would do anything to avoid confinement. Fortunately, she was in detention where her decisions were being made for her because her thought processes tended to careen out of control. Faced with the same choice at home she would have done something desperate such as running, escaping through heavy drug usage, or "hooking up" (establishment of some type of relationship) with someone in order to escape her assignment. Although not suicidal, she had a self-destructive history and was watched very closely.

One of Tonya's favorite expressions was "been there, done that." When you read her essay you will agree that she did not exaggerate. CHARGES: bench warrant served, robbery, grand larceny attempt, battery, burglary

TONYA: ESSAY #6

"My name is Tonya. I am seventeen years old and was born a year after my mom and dad moved here in the late seventies.

The apartment complex we lived in had all my extended family living there and I felt very secure and happy. I am so glad I had those five years before it all ended.

"My mom and dad were having problems which stemmed from an affair my mother was having. This really upset the whole family. It got so bad my father left and then I really started to hate my mother because I saw things in the house I shouldn't have seen as a little girl. She got pregnant with this man and when the newborn arrived none of us got any attention but her.

"I got into every kind of mischief I could and eventually had to be sent to live with my dad. It was good there but I still missed having a mother. I wanted to stay with this neighborhood lady and when Dad was against that I started going wild. Gangs, sex, drugs, and whatever interested me were my life at the tender age of twelve. If Dad interfered I would call the cops and say he was hitting me!

"All this eventually caught up with me and the judge decided to try sending me out of town to Grandma. She was old and just couldn't cope with my wild nature. She sent me back home and I jumped into the drug scene with no fear!

"My probation officer became alarmed and had me confined because of a dirty U.A. (urine analysis). That lasted for a few months and then it was back to the old life.

"I didn't care at all. No respect for people or their things. If I saw something I liked it was mine. I just took what I wanted. I looked bad, tattoos all over my body. I dared people to mess with me. I had money, gold draped all over my body, and drugs for sale if you had the price!

"A blast of reality hit me when coming out of a drug overdose, still in a haze, the nurse informed me I was pregnant. This severely changed my life. I had to stop using drugs! I desperately needed help and support but the "happy" father left me when the baby started to show and I was on my own.

"Mia, my beautiful baby was born in my ninth month but only lived for five hours. I've never been so sad in my life! Jose Seko, Mia's father, wasn't there for us but he did start coming around later to comfort me because "he heard how hard I was taking the whole thing." He was around so much we got back together--long enough for him to get me pregnant again! What was I thinking of? That he'd stay by my side this time? Wrong! I wanted him forever but another girl caught his eye.

"I just couldn't go through the pain of having a second baby on my own and had an abortion just after my fourth month. I didn't want to but it was something I just felt I had to do.

"It hurts to think about why God took my baby Mia and it hurts to think about giving up my second baby but I pray I did the right thing. I pray things will start to make sense for me now."

COMMENTARY

Her cousin's father had just been charged and convicted of murder because he shook a younger child to death. He was caught through a tip from a disgruntled relative and the inept way he tried to dispose of the body in the desert. Both Tonya and her seventeen- year-old cousin Lupe realized they needed to separate themselves from their natural families, but knew it would be a painful process.

They also grasped the urgency of being free of gang affiliation, a separation extremely difficult for Tonya. Her cousin had deeper ties to her family; she was very close to her mother and an aunt. She wanted to continue to have a relationship with her mother, even though she'd been convicted of complicity in the death of her little sister. Lupe and Tonya developed a deep bond during this time and were a very necessary support system for each other.

Tonya admitted to having a "mean streak" which often precluded her from making good judgments in critical situations. Her schooling had been sketchy, disjointed, leaving huge gaps in her skills development in such important subjects areas as English, mathematics, science, and social studies. All vital for success on the GED. Drugs would always loom as an ominous danger to her well-being because they served as a crutch for so long. She has plenty of drive and determination and is a self-described "gutsy one." What will the coda bring?

MATTHEW'S STORY

Matthew, not particularly imposing physically is extremely articulate, and writes and draws very well. He is African/American, just under six feet tall, medium build. He considers himself very macho and works diligently to display the bluster and braggadocio of the hardened, vicious gangbanger.

Matthew was born in the Mason Park public housing section of town. One of the meanest, toughest, and most violent gangs in the area. Mason Park gang members backed up their bravada with ample muscle, either guns or sheer physical intimidation.

Matthew was very proud of Mason Park and hell-bent on proving that he was tough enough to belong there. An excellent, talented student, he was extremely likable when he shed his macho facade. His caseworker feared his gang deeply influenced him and would ultimately be Matthew's nemesis--in the end. He had fathered a child and had a very close relationship with his mother, but barely mentioned either of them in any of our conversations. He bluntly stated: "Mason Park is where it's at!" exuberant in his singleminded focus. CHARGES: assault police officer, possession firearm, display firearm, violation probation, possession stolen property

MATTHEW: ESSAY #7

"My life as Matthew B. all started back in fifth grade when gangbangin' was the only way to go and they were trying to rope me in. It was a bangin' hood on the west side and had all ages, sizes, sexes, and makes (descriptions).

"I was a real good school boy at first, ignoring my brothers, who were the ones doing dirt back then. They sold the dope, bussed (roughed up) mothafuckas, robbed, and rode with O.G. gangstas while earning their reputation. Me, on the other hand, went to school every day, staying away from the crack selling, all that shit. My brothers were always complaining about the packed jails.

"You know I started as a good kid but my brothers just

wouldn't let me be so friendly, so nice, such a good guy. I tried to fight their persuasion, the gang influence, all the propositions of the hood, stay away from peer pressure and remain a school boy. It wasn't going to happen!

"At age nine the hood took me undah! I started cuttin' school and started slangin' (selling) dope. Come up and wanted a little mo'. Bitches came a dime a dozen. Riden' with niggaz twice my age! Shooting in other neighborhoods and jackin' (taking from) mothafuckas too! Put it like this, if it ain't ruff it ain't me. Everything illegal...I was there!

"Fucking women my mom's age. Grown-ups respected me. O.G.'s even look up at me. My street name Boogee, is a known nickname people fear. Me and my brothers did whatever we wanted to do. We sold dope together, used dope together.

"Now since I was so smart I was a good con-man. I could out-slick anybody. I was high rolling at nine. But dope dealing? I didn't really get into it too deep. My thing was jacking (stripping a car, wheels, etc.), stealing, and selling goods.

"Age fifteen I had done everything that was illegal. So now I'm a car thief. I steal car rims and tires, stereos, guns, cellular phones, and anything that might be in a car. If it's there it's mine. Me and my homie, Big Marty, went out every night to steal. The day when I turned seventeen they nailed me. On my birthday.

"Now I'm in juvenile detention and Big Marty is at home with Lil Marty still doing the wild thing. My mom's not surprised that I'm in here and neither am I.

"I got a son out there and one on the way. Well, I guess that's life. Peace."

COMMENTARY

I asked him what that last paragraph was supposed to mean and he refused to elaborate except to admit that he missed them. His true character and his needy feelings were too heavily encased in the macho facade to which he tenaciously clung. I felt I'd never really penetrated his armor. More than anything else, he was totally intent on portraying himself as "bad." I wondered when or if his facade would crumble.

One day he remained after class to talk. I sensed he might have something to confide, so I spoke with him when the classroom emptied. He said he was being assigned to this camp in the mountains, but I shouldn't be surprised if he was released before that. Mason Park was using its "muscle" to secure his release and people, including the judge were listening. I told him that was impressive and relayed the story to his caseworker. She said Matthew had delusions of grandeur and would be off to camp within the month. School ended the next week and Matthew probably knew I would never hear the conclusion to his macho story.

RIV'S STORY

"Slangin' cane" (selling marijuana) plays a major role in Riv's life. Recently turned eighteen, he has very light skin, Afro-American facial features, and red hair kept in "corn rows." One of the aides who knew his family background described him as a trick baby, a child born to a prostitute whose father is rarely known.

He was raised in an intermutual setting with his mother, grandmother, aunts, and uncles and all of their siblings. He refers to the entire group as "family." When he uses the term parents, he is referring to all the adults in the home.

This is a fairly common living arrangement among the poor of any ethnic background. Incredibly, often fourteen people shared his grandmother's little two bedroom, one bath home. Riv, who has never had any privacy in his living accommodations, was amazed that detainees complained about juvenile detention. He didn't particularly like the food and missed his lady, but he found the cottages comfortable and actually seemed to enjoy the camaraderie of his cottage cellmates.

His childhood mirrors the home life many of the students recall of their early years. In his story one can see the different transformations in Riv's life as he goes from a carefree child

absorbed with his recreational pursuits at the sport's complex to slangin' cane on the streets. Throughout this time he maintained a fondness for lifting weights and his body showed the results.
CHARGES: possession of controlled substance, violation probation, curfew, possession stolen property

RIV: ESSAY #8

"I am the youngest of two children. My sister and I were raised with two cousins by our grandmother and our mothers in this little two bedroom house. We also had four uncles and three aunties living with us most of the time. It was easy growing up where I was staying. I did not have to worry about anything as a little boy.

"Our parents were very beloved people towards all of us in the family. They made sure all the kids were sent off to school each day in order to get an education. I always enjoyed the activities at school and especially the sports because I was usually the best at whatever I did. I put forth my best effort because everyone told me there was an athlete inside me.

"I had good grades in elementary and junior high school because I wanted to learn. However, the older I got the more I knew what was going on in the streets. So now, this is where the hangin' out started with my homies.

"We had a saying, 'there is only one shade', meaning Bloods,
our gang association. The Bloods all used to be together every day as a big team, playing football, doing acrobatics, and teaching one another. We also belonged to the recreation center where we participated in every sport and league they offered. We went to camps and tournaments all over Southern California and other places.

This is what a youngster should have the chance to experience while growing up.

"As I got a little more mature things got a little more rowdy. Rowdy like gangbanging, fighting, smoking marijuana, and hangin' out. At that time I was being hardheaded, thinking those were the right things to do. We just thought we were having fun!

"You had to have money and it was made slangin' cane. In order to have nice things, new clothes, I had to sell dope every day. Nothing changed as far as school or activities. What I did on the street was a hobby, something to do after school each day. Fast lane living!"

COMMENTARY

Riv is remarkable in many ways. After the school district tested him, he was certified as a special education student with special educational needs. Riv's special classes were in a smaller setting with a reduced pupil/teacher ratio, accenting material geared to his attainment level in all subjects areas with mainstreaming to regular classes when suitable. He did well and was on track for a special education degree. But he felt a certain stigma was attached to a special education degree and reasoned a GED track would be more beneficial. He recognized the value of an education, doggedly determined to get a degree.

Unfortunately his gang affiliation is absolute, very important to him, and a connection he could or would not easily relinquish. Education and gang affiliation play a recurrent melody in his life. Obviously, the two are not compatible. The looming question is, which will play the dominant role in his life?

CHANGING ENVIRONMENT

When parents suspect their child is having gang related problems, they believe a change of environment offers the solution to the problem. This may seem to be a constructive option for a teen confronting negative associations in their neighborhood, but such change could be prove too traumatic. Teenagers especially need to belong, find a niche; this is a paramount and basic need which if not met, can lead to harmful and self-destructive associations.

DANE'S STORY

Dane's life is an example of such traumatic change. His

family freshly relocated, Dane found these neoteric surroundings hostile, necessitating many difficult adjustments. He is the poster child for the troubled teenager. As Timothy Williams describes such a teen: "He is a gang member. He comes from a single-parent home. His only male role models have been fellow gangbangers. He drinks, smokes cigarettes, has sex, and at times has robbed, beaten and even shot people" (L.A.Times, "A Youth in Trouble," 1-3-95).

At age 15, Dane relocated at a very crucial time in his life. Adjustment problems have plagued him ever since. His commanding presence and visceral image exact respect from all detainees. He is Caucasian with very light blonde hair, a smooth, clear complexion, massive arms and upper body, and a slight scowl permanently imprinted on his face; the look of someone you dare not betray.

His story offers valuable understanding and insight into the relocation process for a teenager. His gang has a viselike grip on Dane and he works diligently to portray the similitude of the hardened gangster a la Cagney or Dilinger. CHARGES: gang enhancement, DUI alcohol, no drivers license, false information, obstructing police officer, curfew violation

DANE: ESSAY #9

"Since I moved here my life has changed drastically. Where I used to live I was never in big trouble with the law. Now I have been locked up three times since I moved here two years ago. I am currently detained and waiting to serve six to eight months in the state facility.

"When people say this is just a small city and doesn't have nearly as many gang problems as big cities they are totally underestimating this place. I never had problems like this before. Since moving here the gangs have been all around me.

"Since ninth grade I started hanging out with a gang called Little Mocho. Getting jumped into this gang is not what led me to trouble, it may have helped, but it has always been my attitude. I just keep getting into more and more serious trouble.

For some reason I just have lived a different lifestyle in this place.

"This is a smaller city and you have to keep the image or reputation for being hard, being a gangster more seriously. You get to know a lot of people and even the different high school students get to know you or at least your reputation.

"Where I was from no one even noticed you unless you were a killer. Kids there didn't really worry about much. You didn't have be nasty and try to impress people.

"This past year I have been getting into a lot of trouble and haven't even bothered to attend school. My attitude is that getting drunk or high is all life has to offer!"

COMMENTARY

Though repeatedly warned not to write in gang style symbols, he would revert back to that style continuously. When corrected he protested in calo' (slang language of Hispanic gangs) claiming we impeded his progress and demanded we leave him alone. A master of intimidation, he used it extensively on his peers, attempted to use his "skill" on teachers and court staff as well.

His academic progress essentially ended with his move to this area. School became secondary in his life, yet he managed to score well on the GED pretest. With skill amplification during his state confinement, he should have acquired the expertise necessary to pass the GED test.

Ed Humes, author of <u>No Matter How Loud I Shout: A Year in the Life of Juvenile Court</u>, writes: "There is fear we have of the violence we're seeing now in some of our children: We're becoming a nation afraid of our children."[*] He discusses the need to humanize children instead of demonizing them. Teens like Dane are easy to demonize because of their intimidating physical stature and deliberately practiced harsh/menacing demeanor. Several court studies indicate the lives of teen

---

[*] Simon & Shuster, 1966

gangsters are often nasty, brutish, and short lived. Dane appeared to be working feverishly to fulfill that prophesy.

KATRINA"S STORY

Many of the juvenile detainees have a family history of several generations of gang involvement. Katrina has been exposed to the gang syndrome her entire life. The offspring of a Caucasian father and Hispanic mother, Katrina refers to her mother, one cousin, and herself as the only "normal ones" in her entire family.

Katrina, a small, light-olive-skinned teen with a slight Hispanic accent, has long cascading black hair, several large tattoos on her arms, and gang inscriptions on the knuckles of both hands. She refers to herself as a frog (girl with low morals) who likes to play the game (criminal activity). She owns a gat (gun) but insists it is just for her own protection, does not like la key (police); and is really close to only one person, her jefita (mother).

Katrina says she is looking at a bullet (one year in custody) primarily because she likes bumping titties (fighting) too much. Almost eighteen when released, she says she will be gang related por vida (forever) as an adult and they better not try to change that while she is in custody. CHARGES: shoplifting, possession stolen property, obstructing police officer, drug paraphernalia.

"When I was little we used to live in a bangin' hood (neighborhood) with my cousins and all our family. We did bad things like steal from people and from the Seven/Eleven stores. My one cousin was a locote (crazy dude) who was always setting us up to do the game (steal). He would be in the background doing ceramics (inhalants) and calling us pinchis (chickens/afraid) if we didn't do it.

"It was getting out of controlla (control) and we had to move, so we picked out a nice part of town and left most of my family behind. Our new home was nice but the schools were so hard that my grades were always F's and D's. My school troubles were not just with my grades but also with the other girls in the school. I was always in a fight with one of them.

"When I finally got into middle school (sixth through eighth grade) I had lost all interest in an education. My only interests were drugs, sex, chingasos (fighting), and hangin' with my homies in the set. It was going to happen anyway so in ninth grade one of my uncles, an O.G., had me courted into the gang. All my family was in it too.

"My aunts and uncles were all chucos (veterans of the gang) and we controlled things in the hood. My father was in prison most of this time but he would talk to my family about prison and the gang he was in. It's crazy. The only normal ones are my jefita, my cousin Marilyn, and me. We try to avoid the G-springs (gangster ride), hold a job, and avoid trouble. It seems like I always slip back into drugs, using and selling clucks (cocaine smokes) and other things.

"I started getting into trouble at school with drugs and fighting; me and my friends jumped this one skinhead girl and they sent me to a reform school. I didn't like it and I was not getting along real well at home so I started running away from home to hang out with my friends. My P.O. had put me on six months probation and when I got into some more trouble with drugs they brought me here. I'm looking at a little less than a bullet (one year) in the state institution and perhaps a very short time on parole until I'm eighteen. They better not try to tell me that I can't have anything to do with gangs because that is not how it works. My gang por vida!"

COMMENTARY

Katrina has a violent temper, may be a compulsive thief, is a drug addict, and by her own admission has little control over her sexual appetite. She is compulsive in nearly every facet of her life but feels she is perfectly normal. Moreover, she is extremely resentful of counselors who try to motivate her to change.

A staff person was temporarily assigned to her case until Katrina's state confinement. Even with this litany of problems, she felt Katrina's personality profile matched the other girls with one exception; the others had become adept at telling people what they wanted to hear while Katrina was always totally open and forthright.

Might there be a way to work with this quality of openness and burgeoning honesty to guide Katrina on a healthier, or at least less self-destructive path? Katrina's frankness should be nourished and thoroughly exploited for her betterment. While her self-absorption with gangs seems totally out of focus and disconcerting it may not be such a stumbling block that she can't function in a legitimate life setting. She is an impatient youngster who has been emotionally wounded by a wide variety of life's encounters. Yet she somehow exudes a warmth, though in a bewilderingly erratic manner, that seems to indicate she is eager to work on her problems. Do we have the tools to help kids like Katrina?

A NATIONAL NIGHTMARE

The gang problem in our nation is undeniably a national nightmare affecting all segments of society but most particularly the poor. Politicians from Washington to the local community are demanding a crackdown on, and harsher penalties for, gang enhanced crime. Gang members are often portrayed as incurably heinous; driven by violence and illicit drugs. Somehow we have to stop the bloody rampage of gang violence that has claimed so many of our nations' young people.

In Los Angeles, city and county prosecutors have joined in legal action to ban any public association of even two gang members. Los Angeles Superior Court Judge William C. Beverly on Friday, August 30, 1997 approved a preliminary injunction against fifteen reputed 18th street gang members pending a full trial. The court order "bans the defendants from standing, sitting, walking, driving or appearing anywhere in the target area with a known 18th street gang member. They also are prohibited from possessing drugs, drug paraphernalia, beepers, cellular phones, police scanners and weapons." (L.A.Times, 8-30-97).

In the same article Governor Pete Wilson of California

praised the court decision, saying "we are sending a clear message (that) we will use all available tools to curb illegal gang activity...We cannot call ourselves a civilized society if our homes become prisons to innocent citizens who live in fear." The "message" going out to the communities is one prosecutors hope will cripple recruiting efforts in the area by keeping gang members off the streets. This is an ominous task and one that will not be accomplished easily or quickly. The long-term success of this latest initiative is being anxiously and optimistically watched throughout the nation.

Professor John Dilulio of Princeton University has initiated a program which he calls the "four-M" approach. He borrows from both the liberal and conservative views on juvenile crime, talking about the devastating impact of poverty and joblessness which appeals to liberals, and warning of the impact of out-of-wedlock births, and single parent-headed households which conservatives love to hear.

Dilulio, like so many in the field, feels that youth crimes at the front end call for preventive measures while crimes at the back end generally call for incarceration. He travels to inner-city Philadelphia to work with local clergy and church volunteers on front-end responses to juvenile crime. Here he applies the four M's; monitoring, mentoring, ministering, and finally establishing a sense of moral obligation to these needy children.

"Monitoring by adult volunteers in Philadephia's Youth Aid Panel program tailors punishment to fit the crime and the personal conditions of first-time youth offenders who used to fall between the cracks of the probation system" (Clarence Page, Las Vegas Sun, 2-17-98). This is followed by mentoring (taking at-risk children "under wing") which has produced some impressive statistics: 1] 46 percent less likely to initiate drug use 2] 27 percent less likely to use alcohol 3] 33 percent less likely to commit assault 4] 50 percent less likely to skip school. Ministering is credited with raising school grades and attendance and helping establish a sense of "moral obligation" that gets grown-ups involved with these youth.

Columnist Clarence Page noted similar approaches are showing positive results in other cities, most dramatically in

Boston, "where kids with too much time on their hands are targeted by police, prosecutors and community volunteers... There is some good news happening in America's streets. Legislators should listen and learn, or just leave bad enough alone" (Ibid.).

The body of evidence is growing and it points to the desperate need for adults in the community to become involved in a meaningful way with youthful offenders. Churches and community-minded service organizations can be extremely effective in helping these children who have essentially been abandoned by their parents. If we approach front-end crime diligently we can make an impact on the devastation caused by poverty and joblessness and stem the flow of out-of-wedlock births and the inexorable single-parent household.

Chapter 3

PATTERNS REPEATED
Facing Tough Odds

American society is committed to the idea that the most critical factor in a young person's life is their peer group. While this premise has validity studies show that older children with close ties to their parents are less likely to contemplate suicide, have sex at an early age, smoke cigarettes, drink, take drugs, or become violent (<u>Journal of the American Medical Association</u>, Sept. 1997). Professor Michael Resnick, University of Minnesota, writes: "As a culture we've bought into the idea that the peer group swallows our kids alive once they make it into adolescence. Teenagers are very skillful at convincing us that we have become irrelevant in their lives. But parents' expectations, values, and connectedness are fundamentally important" (<u>Raleigh News & Observer</u>, 9-10-97).

The myth that one's teenage peers, rather than parents, impact most strongly on teen behavior has been debunked. Examples set by the parents are strong factors in influencing teens on the brink of adulthood. My long experience as a school principal supports the fact that children living in unstable households are more apt to drop out of school, exhibit emotional distress, violate the law, and abuse drugs or alcohol.

Abused children, much more prone to emotional problems, often end up in juvenile court. As adults, they're far more apt to become abusive parents. The alarming fact is that the most frequent child abuser, by a significant margin, is the natural parent! Statistics released by WE CAN, INC.[*] indicate 90 percent of juvenile offenders and adult prisoners claim abuse as children (<u>Las Vegas Review Journal</u>, 9-21-97). According to the

---

[*] WE CAN, INC. is extant in all states. Its mission is child abuse prevention/improvement of the quality of life for all children.

Nevada Division of Child and Family Services, abuse by a natural parent accounts for 82 percent of the substantiated cases in Nevada (Same source). Children must be protected from inappropriate parents, and this must be society's main focus. Only then can we begin to curtail abusive behavior, which has far-reaching ramifications on all levels of society.

Courts throughout America have traditionally leaned toward keeping the original family intact, giving the natural parents liberal opportunities to raise their children. Court expectations are that drug treatment, counseling, or other professional intervention will eventually correct aberrant, dangerous parental behavior.

Results dispute these barren expectations. Study after study affirms Thomas Sowell's conclusions (Las Vegas Review Journal, Fall, 1997) that we must get "children away from parents who have repeatedly battered, raped or tortured them...The very man who designed California's scheme to reunite families through counseling--Professor Michael Wald of Stanford University--was unable to find hard evidence that it was working when he studied the data and issued his report some years ago."

NATIONAL CRISIS

We are facing a crisis in the poor communities of this nation. To raise children with a reasonable chance for success will require many things; employment opportunities for parents, networking between responsible adults working in the community, creation of a successful school environment, a safe, stimulating learning and recreational program in neighborhood community centers, and active, involved religious institutions.

"The 7.1 million children growing up in poor communities today face tough odds! Research predicts that they are at greater risk of being sick and having inadequate health care; of being parents before they complete school; of being users of easily available drugs; of being exposed to violence; and of being incarcerated before they are old enough to vote. Although poor neighborhoods include individuals and families with extraordinary resilience and strength, too many kids growing up in such environments will reach adulthood unprepared to parent, to work, and to contribute to society" (Kids Count Data Book,1997). Kids Count is a project of the Annie E. Casey Foundation, which is recognized nationally for its efforts to track the status of children in the United States and provide benchmarks of child well-being.

A study of admissions to a pediatric intensive care unit indicates that child abuse cases "had the highest hospital charges and the highest mortality rates. Medical bills averaged $35,641 per case, and even so, 70 percent died and 60 percent of survivors had severe residual morbidity" (Child Abuse and Neglect, The International Journal, Aug.1997). Too often a helpless child is returned to the parent only to suffer further abuse. Sadly, in far too many cases, this results in either a permanently disabled or dead child! It is a blight on society that bureaucratic and legalistic roadblocks often prevent healthy couples from being allowed to adopt abused children. The legislative and legal processes must be accelerated to effectively confront these dilemmas.

The desperate needs of the abused child demand our immediate attention and immediate solutions. Communities are simply not dealing effectively with this national crisis. They need more effective elucidation from professionals in all facets of the community. Certainly, they need more financial and legal assistance, and better trained and more aware professionals: social and case workers, psychologists, physicians, judges, law enforcement. Fundamental to all of this is an increased emphasis on parental education.

The stories in this chapter reveal the devastating effects that an impoverished emotional environment inflicts on a child. Notice that these stories are acutely devoid of the typical fond memories of childhood most of us still cherish as adults. These youngster's stories illustrate the alarming reality of the psychological abuse and family dysfunctions they've encountered daily. These are the children who frequent our juvenile institutions throughout the nation.

As you read these essays, bear in mind that "45 percent of arrested 9-to-12-year-old children investigated by child welfare had an incarcerated parent. Ninety percent of Sacramento's twenty "costliest" children in placement, of any age, had an incarcerated parent" (<u>Common Ground</u>, Nov.1997).* Only 1.2 percent of all the children in the United States have been investigated for physical abuse, while the figure is 62 percent of children 9 to 12 who were investigated by child welfare. Incarceration of one or both parents gives these children the perception that somehow this is normal, almost a naturally occurring circumstance, creating a pattern likely to be repeated.

With unflinching honesty the painful details of their life are recalled. These stories remind me of the Italian expression, "<u>Dove</u> <u>sona</u> <u>I</u> <u>bel</u> <u>momenti</u>?" Where are the lovely moments? For most, their "lovely moments" are those of escape: drugs, alcohol, sex, or other 'highs' they might invoke via guns or cars. Guns and cars serve to empower them, and are often abhorently exploited with disastrous results!*

ROBERTO'S STORY

Roberto, 17, constantly laments the lack of a male figure in his life. A handsome young man at five-foot-six inches, a little shorter than his peers, but well proportioned and very meticulous about his personal appearance. His hair was coifed in the latest style which even the detention haircut couldn't mask.

Although he tried very hard to fit in with the other boys in his unit, he could never be an accepted member of his group. The truth is he worked <u>too</u> <u>hard</u> at being friendly and helpful; even staff contrived ways to keep him at arm's length. He was not a 'sissy boy' (which his peers labeled those physically weak), and could hold his own physically with almost all the other boys. But everyone perceived him as being too needy which, unfortunately, proved self-defeating.

Roberto is likely to re-enact the same role with his child that

---

* <u>Common</u> <u>Ground</u> *is a newspaper of the New England Association of Child Welfare Commissioners and Directors.*

his father pursued with him. He feels a tremendous pressure to "do the right thing" for his lady and his unborn child, yet he imitates his father in discharging his obligations. What are his chances of breaking the cycle? CHARGES: possession controlled substance, possession narcotic paraphernalia, possession with intent to sell, violation curfew

ROBERTO: ESSAY #11

"From the day I was born until about my fifth year I don't remember anything. I was told about an accident I was in that supposedly resulted in my having a faint memory since then.

"At the age of five my dad became more interested in drugs than his family so essentially he was lost to me at a very young age. Abandoned, I and my entire family were brought to the streets. We had no food, clothes, home, or money. I lived with my family in our little blue car until we had to sell it to get money. After that we lived out of shelters until my grandma accepted us in her house.

"Mom said my dad would come looking for us because he didn't want to pay child support. He would abuse my mom and even us kids so we had to move to another city and start over again. My mom found an apartment which was our first real home. It wasn't bad if you accepted the fact you would probably get beat up every day and harassed in order to go to school. That's about it for my early years. Does that help explain why I'm in here?

"We received a pretty good education because mom would never let us cut school. She always fought for us and tried to make us live right. She even found us a house we could afford. We were on welfare and it helped us get the house and get through hard times.

"In the fourth grade my brother introduced me to marijuana. That was the first time I had ever smoked or messed with drugs but they hooked me and I've been doing them every since. About this time we decided to move, we're always moving, and new schools come into play. I meet new friends and, with the drugs and all, slide into the thug life.

"I still managed to get into high school four years later, and that is where I start seriously thinking about girls. At this time girls, drugs, and football are the main things on my mind. I'm living good because Mom's off welfare and my grandmother is back with us taking care of the house and cooking great food.

"At seventeen I meet the most beautiful girl in the world. She's sixteen, very attractive, and has a bright future ahead of her. I feel like she loves me! We start a big romance and immediately she becomes pregnant. We talk it over and decide, even though it means interrupting everything, I need to go out and raise money for her abortion. She doesn't want to quit her studies and give up on a career and I support her on that.

"While trying to raise money I got busted for trafficking and landed here in juvenile detention. That wasn't my first time in detention, so I was real lucky to get released to an outside program...which I screw up! So here we are. She is pregnant. I'm locked up. All I can do is work on my GED and hope for the best.

"My life is basically shitty. I lost my dad to drugs and my grandfather died when I was thirteen. He was really the only father I ever had. Now, I'm going to be a father. I need to quit the thug life and find a way to get out of here so I can help raise my baby!"

COMMENTARY

There is much to analyze here--to read between the lines. Roberto is clearly in conflict. He has had no male role model, but he has a mother who obviously cares, and has showed persistence in sustaining her family. Obviously he has been sustained by his mother's display of strength; "She always fought for us." One of Roberto's favorite expressions is 'it's crunch time' (critical) which it truly is for him. He recognizes his responsibility in "screwing up." Will he manifest the determination to meet his obligation or will he succumb to "thug life" and follow in his father's shadow, which he described as 'druggin and runnin'?

He needs to focus on education in order to secure a stable

job and provide for his family. At this point education seems less compelling than other things because the rewards are protracted. Roberto, like many detainees, tends to look for the quick fix. But, the GED is his best chance to achieve meaningful and deep-rooted success in his life.

JOHN'S STORY:

Repeating patterns are starting to surface in John's life: At close to six-feet, of medium build, and long stringy brown hair, John has a very pale complexion and gang tattoos decorate his hands and one arm. Caucasian with Hispanic gang affiliation, John's early childhood was marked by frequent hospital visits, brief stays at Child Haven for abused and neglected children, while he was shuttled back and forth between parents. Both parents avoided their responsibilities toward their children, unequipped to properly raise a family. The consequences for John are unfortunately predictable.

After divorcing, his mother was overwhelmed and immediately released her youngest child to the court system. Thus, John "lost" a little brother and his father. John's mother used most of the available social services as she tried to raise her children. Although the programs were a lifeline, ultimately she couldn't deal with the complexities and challenges of child-rearing in a gang-infested environment. For her children, their gang affiliation became the most important factor in their lives.

The conundrum of conceiving a child and then being unable to cope with the responsibility is manifest. When John's first girlfriend became pregnant, her parents intervened and separated them. John felt totally victimized by her parents, denying his responsibility. He feels his mother is his only certainty, and holds her in high esteem. Yet he feels he has failed her. CHARGES: no drivers license, possession stolen plates, possession controlled substance, evading police officer, possession deadly weapon.

JOHN: ESSAY #12

"After I was born I had major physical problems but I don't know what exactly. They had tubes in me but after a few days passed I was all right. Then about eight months after my birth I was rushed to the hospital for something else and they even told my mother that I wasn't going to make it. Why they told her that I don't know because I am still here.

"I have two brothers and four sisters. At the age of seven years we all did pretty good but then our family broke up; my father and mother separated. Everyone but my youngest brother stayed with my mom. My dad kept everything but the station wagon and told my mother she had to get an apartment.

"After we moved, she met a man named Pascual and started living with him in our apartment. One day my sister Jeanine and I got into a physical fight with him. When Mom came home in the morning she woke me and my sister up and took us to our father's house. I was kinda happy because I could go back to my old school with all my friends.

"My father was an alcoholic and he didn't really care how I did in school, so I got into fights a lot and my grades started going down. So at age twelve I was ordered back to my mother's place.

"She already got remarried and didn't have much time for me so I started hanging around gangs. We did bad stuff like skipping school and drinking beer. My mother did all she could to discipline me, but I didn't care and kept on doing bad things.

"One day I just decided to run away from home and was gone for several months. When I came back home my mom had to take me to counseling. That didn't work so she moved me in with this Christian family she knew. They went to church three times a week. I managed to stay there for five months and then moved back with Mom.

"After I moved back everything stayed pretty much the same except now I was smoking pot and using drugs. At thirteen I met this girl named Lolita and we sort of fell in love. Her dad didn't like me at all so one day we decided to run away together. They found us two weeks later and she went back home. I stayed where we were.

"Two weeks passed. I saw Lolita and she decided to go with me again. We spent a week together and then her parents came and got her again. This time they sent her to Mexico. She was pregnant, and I have never seen her since.

"After about five more months I moved back with my mother. Nothing had changed with me, and at fifteen I got arrested for some burglaries and was put on probation. I finished probation after two years. It was supposed to be six months but I kept getting into minor scrapes. They finally gave me a citation saying I had completed probation.

"I messed up real bad after completing my probation and got put in here for having a concealed weapon and three PCP sticks (AKA angel dust). I'm seventeen and have a child on the way with a girl named Evelyn. I'm hurting inside; longing for my unborn child, my girlfriend, and my mother. I just want one more chance to change for my family and to prove myself to the important people in my life."

COMMENTARY

"One more chance" is the rallying cry for so many teens in similar circumstances. And they deserve that. Not yet adult, with no skills, they already feel defeated by life! With deep drug and alcohol problems, and heavy affiliation with gangs, how can they convince the authorities that leniency would result in a healthy change? What type of professional intervention could possibly work with this young man and others like him?

He desperately needs occupational skills to succeed in even a menial job in the work force. Sadly he fails to grasp the significance of education in his future. Without an intense amount of pressure, he will not pursue this path.

One possibility--the judge could decree the successful completion of the GED as a condition for his release. The problem--when he turns eighteen he'll most likely be released whether or not he has completed it. Then he and his criminal behavior will become a problem for the adult institutions.

"Children who live in poverty from the time before they are born until they become adults are less likely to grow up to become productive adults. Their development is impaired and the long-term costs to them and to society are great. The relationship between poverty and impaired physical, social, and emotional development is well documented." (Gustavsson-Segal, Critical Issues in Child Welfare)*

FEMINIZATION OF POVERTY

And what about his young girlfriend and their offspring? One immediate factor to consider is the "feminization of poverty" (Pearce, D., Urban and Social Change Review, 1978). The feminization of poverty reflects the trend toward more women, particularly those who are single heads of households, living in poverty. The average income for female-headed families in 1988 was $16,077 compared with married couples with $37,069 per year (U.S.Bureau of the Census, 1990). What hope is there for them as they begin their journey through life? What type of immediate intervention is needed? By whom? What social institution or agency will accept this challenge? Our nation must address these problems, because they are patterns repeated ad nauseam. Solutions to the plight of teenagers are desperately needed now!

These teens drift into a destructive lifestyle that soon becomes the total focus of their being. The ramifications of their actions-gang involvement, dealing drugs, or stealing cars--are not apparent to them until their involvement is so deep that the impact of negative behaviors has palpable consequences.*

The staggering rate of unemployment in gang-immersed communities is proclaimed as the most significant factor in the epidemic of violence. The Los Angeles Police Department Census Bureau in their 1997 report declares that unemployment and per capita income were the most significant factors in gang-related homicides between 1988 and 1992. In communities with

---

*　　_____　Sage Publications, 1994

unemployment at between fourteen and sixteen percent, they had 125 to 175 gang homicides per 100,000 population! This is about fifteen times the killing rate compared to communities where unemployment ran a modest four to seven percent.

The average delinquent's motivation for gang involvement is complex. Two main reasons are evident: Some genuinely feel the need for protection, while others lack strong family ties that might preclude the drift toward gangs. There are many reasons for joining. Most teens fail to realize the extent of their commitment when they take the initial step.

SMITTY'S STORY

Smitty failed to realize the consequences of gang involvement until someone passed a gun and ordered him to use it. Smitty, well over six feet, is an imposing figure, with a body enhanced by much weight training. He credits his detention time with his interest in weights, where he learned the nuances of "lifting". I'm not sure society was well served in this situation. Unless he changes drastically we've enhanced an unstable teen's physical prowess and, thus may have to deal with him as an adversary.

A Caucasian, Smitty's gang is evenly mixed racially: Caucasian, Hispanic, and Afro-Americans. Although physically imposing, Smitty has an understated presence, is never obtrusive or loud, and appears to give his best effort to whatever he is doing. Soon eighteen, he begins a brief interval before entering the adult arena. CHARGES: evading a police officer, obstruction police officer, hit/run reckless driving, false police report, leaving scene, no drivers license, grand larceny attempt, gang enhancement, under influence controlled substance

SMITTY: ESSAY #13

"It all started when I was in the fifth grade and my mom told me a story about how she used to gangbang. She talked about things that happened when she was a teenager and they sounded like fun. She did tell me <u>not</u> to do things like what she did but I didn't listen to that part.

"It was about then when I started doing things that were bound to get me in trouble. I was doing drugs and going around beating up people. I did this for a while and then in seventh grade decided to get jumped into the set I was kicking with. I thought it would be fun and games. I thought wrong! I'd never been in a gang war before and had never shot at anyone before.

"One day I was just kicking it with my homies while they made plans to steal a car and do a drive-by on one of our rivals which I won't name. I was like 'O.K. I'll see you when you get back.' They said uh-uh, I was going with them. When I got into the car my homeboy (gang affiliate) handed me a 9mm gun and said, 'When we get over there just pull the trigger and whatever happens, happens.'

That night my homeboy Slants died. There was not one single thing I could say or do about it!

"A couple of weeks later I happened to steal a car myself because I had to go pick up my homeboy's sister. I picked her up and proceeded down the street when the cops passed me going in the opposite direction. They flipped a U-turn and came back to pull me over. I panicked because I was on speed and tried to get away. Unfortunately the car could not handle the corner and flipped into a ditch. Me and the girl jumped out and tried to run but were caught by the cop.

"So now I wish I would have listened to my mother and just let gangs alone. I'm in here waiting to see what the judge is going to do with me. It's not looking good"

COMMENTARY

Obviously Smitty faces incarceration until he reaches eighteen and is declared an adult. By then he would have served enough time in confinement to conceivably obtain a vocational or some other type educational degree. Although educationally mediocre, he had maintained his standing and has accumulated several high school credits.

The likelihood of his escaping the gang influence on his life is minimal. It was a huge factor in his existence. Smitty's entire being revolves around his "homies." His mother knew the dangers he faced as a gang member, but she could not assert enough influence to dissuade him from joining. Now he will need her guidance and help if he is to escape its clutches and find an appropriate place in society.

Ironically, Smitty did not consider drugs a controlling factor in his life; he felt his drug usage could either be eliminated or channeled into a controlled use of alcohol. Wrong! Speed is highly addictive, an extremely hard habit to eliminate. The use of alcohol is usually considered a contributing factor in the use of speed; definitely not an alternative to use when trying to quit drugs!

Violence plays a debilitating role in those who become wards of the court. Most of these youngsters have a violent history. School archives indicate extensive problems with fighting and self control. Nearly all involvement with gangs is oriented toward violence. The profiles of these young people offer compelling and disturbing insight into a world totally alien to conventional, mainstream America.

Predictably the patterns quickly begin to repeat when youngsters reach their late teens. The most repulsive acts are ones prone to repetition. The Seattle Social Development Project (SSDP) headed by David Hawkins of the University of Washington, recently (Fall 1997) completed a study on 808 ethnically-diverse children aged 10 to 18. Approximately 15 percent of these children joined gangs. The results of this study "tend to support an enhancement model of gang membership which proposes that gangs attract already delinquent children, who become more delinquent while in a gang" (Why Do Kids Join Gangs?, SSDP, HandsNet:HN1699, 11-17-97). Once that imprint is made, the cycle repeats and then re-creates itself. Without massive intervention programs, society will continue to produce youngsters such as those depicted in these essays.

JARROD'S STORY

Jarrod, a black youth, is already considered a potentially

dangerous detainee at seventeen. He has always been in close proximity to violence, which he accepts with a shrug, as a way of life. At five-feet, seven-inches tall, a stocky build, he is well coordinated and excels in all sports. A delight to high-school coaches athletically. In fact, coaches throughout the Valley know him. They shake their heads in consternation when discussing his obvious athletic talent.

Easily influenced, Jarrod would follow a suitable person if given the appropriate circumstances. He has some academic skills but would have to get his GED, which would limit the scope of colleges interested in him--a mute point if he is certified as an adult. Without a record of delinquency he could write his own ticket. Even with this encumbrance many colleges would be happy to accept this multi-talented athlete. CHARGES: Possession controlled substance, possession with intent to sell, drug paraphernalia, gang enhancement, concealed weapon.

JARROD: ESSAY #14

"I was born in a little town in Maine and lived briefly with both of my parents. A month after I was born my mother and father split and went separate ways.

"Me and my father headed South and my Mom went her own way. I grew up around my father and a step-mother I really didn't like. She always told me the opposite of what my father said.

"For eight years I grew up without my real mother until one day my dad had got in some big trouble with a lot of people and the police. He told me that I was going to another city because he had killed a couple of people over his money and I was going to be with my real mom.

"When he told me I was going to be with my real mom I didn't really know who he was talking about because I had never seen my real mother. I was separated from her when I was so little I didn't know who he was talking about.

"Me and my dad pack up and come here. Now, this was not a good sight. I met my real family of four brothers and three sisters. Two of my brothers were in a rival blood gang and two of my sisters in the same gang. Being from a different gang, I didn't feel real comfortable.

"A month later me and my mom got a letter from my stepmother saying my dad was dead. Shot and killed! It really broke me down into pieces.

"Time went by and I started adjusting to life, playing some sports and doing fairly good until I met my cousin. He was from another gang called the Rolling Crips. I started hanging with him, getting high and selling drugs. That landed me in here and I really don't know where I'm heading in life."

COMMENTARY

Sadly, the direction in which he is heading is grim. He is derailed temporarily until he fulfills his time in a confinement facility. His probation officer and the judge will decide if he should be certified to stand trial as an adult and serve incarceration in an adult prison. Jarrod is vulnerable and would undoubtedly make personally destructive associations with adult inmates.

He has some serious charges that include a concealed 9mm automatic pistol, but is relatively unresponsive to any attempts or suggestions geared toward rehabilitation. Throughout his life he has been exposed to extremely destructive lifestyles; for him, they are the norm. His chances of redirecting his life are rapidly eroding. If the courts do not remove him from his present living situation and allow him to be rehabilitated through athletics, he will wind up another grim statistic. Basically a follower, he needs desperately to find the right leader.

GANG LOYALTY

Professor/author Clayton Robarchek of Wichita State University believes that gangs inspire the same kind of loyalty as the charismatic Christians and the Black Muslims. The difference is these religious groups give their members "a sense of accountability to a larger society--the same kind of loyalty that gangs inspire, but with nonviolent values. We should be searching our cities for charismatic leaders in the mold of Martin Luther King, Jr and Malcolm X. Rather than demonizing these leaders and the groups they lead, we need to devise ways to make society's resources available to assist them" (As quoted in article by Faye Fiore, L.A.Times, 11-20-97). Some might question his assertion that Malcolm X was non-violent but the point he makes about the need for developing and encouraging leadership is valid. When an adult outside the family offers solid and stable help it has been my observation that positive results often follow.

Children like Jarrod need concrete guidance in order to make healthy, life-sustaining choices that will help them set and achieve goals. A stable adult in the neighborhood, a minister, teacher, coach, policeman, social worker, or probation officer can be immensely effective in providing concrete assistance in a troubled youth's misguided life.

FAMILY ENVIRONMENT

Growing up in a conflicted home environment such as the ones described in these essays is known to affect relationship formation and views concerning family. Individuals from violent/conflicted families are more likely to become involved in dysfunctional relationships as adults. "Children of all ages need to be cared for, nurtured, intellectually stimulated, loved and taught values if they are to feel good about themselves and become contributing members of society. There is consensus, even among politically diverse groups, that the family provides the best environment for meeting the needs of children" (Gustavsson-Segal, op. cit.).

When the family is not functional and the state must become involved, it too, is often an inadequate caretaker. Schools, social programs, and caring individuals must compensate for stressful environments and troubled families. We cannot ignore the reality of violence in the lives of young people and must respond with renewed vigor to make policy and affect research which will bring solutions to block these repeating patterns.

Chapter 4

DRUG REHABILITATON
Use On Upward Ascendance

As a nation educators, parents, politicians, law enforcement, and the public in general lament the steady increase in juvenile crime, and we must confront hard fact. A major contributor to crime is drug use, which is rising at an incredible, some claim explosive rate. Since the beginning of the nineties the number of juveniles arrested for drug-related crimes has more than doubled. In mid- December, 1996, the FBI released statistics showing that arrests jumped from 64,740 in 1990 to 147,107 by 1995 (L.A.Times, 12-26-96).

Alcohol or other drugs were used by 80 percent of the people behind bars during the commission of the crime for which they are incarcerated. According to the National Center on Addiction and Substance Abuse, N.Y., alcohol played an even bigger role in violent crime than crack or powder cocaine (Las Vegas Sun, 1-9-98). The study found that "1.4 million of the 1.7 million people serving time in the nation's jails and prisons committed crimes while they were high, have a history of drug or alcohol abuse or are in jail for violating drug or alcohol laws."

The National Education Goals Report (1997) substantiated the evidence that drug use is rising at an alarming rate. Their survey showed that an incredible 40 percent of tenth-grade students used drugs during their freshman year. (A similar survey in 1992 had 24 percent of tenth-grade students admitting to drug use.) This astronomical increase in drug use is startling, especially since these students had marked improvement in subjects such as mathematics and science.

DRUG USE EXPLOSION

Retired General Barry R. McCaffrey, the chief of the White House Drug Office, commented that these statistics point to "an explosion in drug use." The Republicans blamed the Clinton Administration for not attacking the drug problem aggressively, and the Clinton administration blamed Republicans for failure to approve the funding level sought for drug interdiction. As both sides point fingers, the drug problem intensifies and expands nationally.

PROFILE OF THE STUDENT DRUG DEALER

Who is the purveyor of drugs in the typical school setting? Generally, that person is a gang member, a drug user, and uses school basically as a place to peddle drugs to other students. This person also indulges in alcohol, cigarettes and marijuana on a regular basis. Further, the portrait includes having sex with one or more partner, and criminal activities, mostly robbery and car theft, sometimes involving the use of guns.

Most students defer to, and perhaps fear, the school drug dealer. They know that he, rarely she, is gang affiliated and will retaliate for any minor perceived betrayal. The Colombia University sponsored National Center on Addiction and Substance Abuse reports that only thirty-seven percent of fifteen-year-old students and a very similar figure of thirty-four percent of seventeen years-olds would report a student selling drugs. Among twelve-year-old students the figure was 74 percent.

Most teens decide to use drugs between the ages of fifteen and seventeen, but there are indications these ages are steadily lowering. Columbia University's NCASA through their Commission on Substance Abuse Among America's Adolescents conducted a survey (August, 1997) showing that substance abuse trends among college students are rooted in behavior beginning in middle school (grades 6, 7, and 8). The survey also disclosed that 56 percent of youth aged 12 to 17 say they have friends who use hard drugs (LSD, cocaine, heroin), up from 39 percent in 1996. The greatest increase was among 12-year-olds. An up-beat comment from Joseph A. Califano, Jr., Chairman of the Colombia Center, declared if students are able to make it to age 21 without using illegal drugs "they are virtually certain never to do so." It's very obvious that we must do much more to eradicate the drug selling gang influence from our high schools!

As young people drift toward gang involvement they must be made aware of the drug connection they will face. Any level of gang association will result in an immediate introduction to drugs, and with that an introduction to a multitude of other socially inappropriate behaviors. What most fail to realize until after they are made (formally admitted to the gang) is that even if they become disillusioned with the gang, severing that relationship will have serious consequences. The gang will likely retaliate for leaving. Tragically, staying may be the safer choice.

As the gang increasingly becomes their personal safety net, it also becomes obvious that gun possession enhances that safety net. To acquire a gun on the street you must barter, usually with drugs. Another way of acquiring a gun is to work through your set (gang). They will frequently target gun shops and other stores which handle guns and ammunition. Even private dwellings suspected of having guns on premise are likely to be targeted for burglary.

Guns have become status symbols among gang members; and the more prolonged their gang association, the more likely they will possess a lethal gun with frightening firepower. Most keep a small pistol, easily hidden, for school and other places when they want to carry heat (a gun) while avoiding detection.

To further profile the student drug dealer: they spend virtually no time in the classroom being 'schooled.' Instead they do their slangin' (selling drugs) on the school premises. While accumulating their 'stash' (money or drugs) they dream of owning a car, (a vintage Chevrolet Impala is a popular choice), and "cruisin with their 'bitches' (girlfriends) down the main drag (street)." Drugs enhance these dreams when they're high. The downward spiral begins when the drugs wear off. Then the stark reality of life confronts them, often producing a hair-trigger mentality. The latter can often result in aggressive anti-social activities, such as brutal fights or shootings.

"SNOW BABIES"

Many of the GED students in detention said their parents used drugs. These students said they were born with a drug addiction (snow babies). The general behavior pattern of the "snow baby" includes: intense restlessness, recoiling from hugs or touches, easily startled by sounds, and difficulty in focusing.

In their teens these behaviors are very apparent. They act impulsively, are inattentive, unable to focus and are easily distracted by noise. Once their attention is diverted by the slightest sight or sound they find it extremely difficult to return to the task on hand.

HOME ENVIRONMENT UNSTABLE

Virtually all have chaotic home environments. It is extremely difficult to ascertain precisely how the impact of drugs in the mother's womb affects the development, socially and psychologically, later in the child's life. In an impoverished household a single parent, overwhelmed with the demands of daily living, creates stress-related behavior in children, and this may well trigger similar classroom responses.

Dr. Ira Chasnoff (University of Illinois) found in his studies of 170 children that "the coke-exposed ones had roughly the same IQ scores at the age of 6 as those whose mothers were clean." The children do fine in a quiet room by themselves says neuroscientist Pat Levitt of the University of Pittsburgh. "But there is no question they have altercations in their brain structure and function which, while not keeping them from learning a task in isolation, could well hurt them in real life" (Newsweek, 9-29-97). A regular school room has a wide variety of distractions which could interfere with the learning process. Studies confirm that I.Q. differences accelerate as such children grow older. Myriad factors determine the outcome of these tests, but fetal exposure is clearly a major factor.

ROGER'S STORY

Roger has run the gamut of self-destructive behavior. When sober he sincerely wishes he could erase his past and move on. He has a serious addiction to "huffing" (inhaling vapors) paint. Huffing did not show on his weekly urine test, enabling him to pass. At the age of seventeen he looks haggard, with deep circles around his eyes, a peaked complexion, and a strange gauntness that defies his youthfulness. His blond hair is usually disheveled and his clothes hang inappropriately on his lanky body.

Extremely sensitive to sound, he had trouble adjusting to a busy classroom: students moved about selecting materials, sharpening pencils, and gathering their resource books. A daydreamer he was frequently not on task and had to be reminded to concentrate on classroom assignments. CHARGES: robbery, urine analysis (U.A.) unknown substance, possession controlled substance, inhaling harmful vapor, curfew

ROGER: ESSAY #15

"My life isn't one of great interest to anybody but myself. I have a great mom and the rest of my family would do anything for me. I always got good grades until I got into high school. My other friends had been doing illegal things since junior high, but not me. In my freshman year I started ditching school and hanging around my homies in the neighborhood gang.

"I eventually got jumped into my set and that started my life of trouble. I began stealing from people, shooting at people, and doing all the things I always saw my friends do and told myself I'd never do.

"I was stealing from my family just to get drugs so I could party with my girlfriend. During this time she got pregnant and that didn't help anything. I didn't know what I was going to do. I just had in mind all the money it was gonna cost. I started robbing people and eventually got arrested.

"I stayed in juvenile detention for a few months, got out, and was assigned to a drug program for counseling and tests. Now this program was making me take three urine tests a week. I knew I'd get caught so the only thing to do was to start huffing paint because it doesn't show up on the tests.

"That started a whole other world of hell. I got addicted to huffing paint and was really close to killing myself from it. I was huffing daily without anybody knowing! After a while they detected it and arrested me for huffing. They locked me up and that is when my girlfriend aborted our baby.

"I got off with a severe warning because my probation officer was out of town and did not handle the charges against me. When she came back into town she called me and she was mad. She had found out I was huffing paint and told me she was going to arrest me. She made the mistake of asking me to turn myself in to her office.

"I thought about it and I just couldn't go back to jail. I had to take a chance so I went on the run for a few months. I knew they would probably catch me eventually and put me back in jail. They did. They caught me but rather than jail they assigned me to this camp for drug addicts. It wasn't too bad and I learned a lot.

"I graduated from the camp in just twelve weeks when they felt I was capable of going back home. I did real good for about two months and then went into reverse and started huffing paint again.

They must have been watching me real close because the minute I stumbled they arrested me.

"I'm back in detention and feeling a lot of regrets. If I had one wish it would be that I never started huffing paint. It could kill me!"

COMMENTARY

Roger's portrait of his family defies the facts. His entire family is involved in the drug scene, including the mother he supposedly "let down." In fact, there is a strong possibility Roger is a "snow baby." A very impulsive student, he could not block out even minor distractions.

We played the radio in the classroom, keeping it closely

monitored. The aim was to help students relax and enjoy music as they did their work. Roger briefly alienated himself from others in the room, complaining about the radio and requesting it be shut off. The other students regarded the radio a major "benny" (extra benefit) Roger considered it a painstaking adjustment. He, like others who have trouble with distractions, had to work diligently on sharpening his ability to concentrate. Huffing paint is so damaging to the brain it's beyond measurement; but Roger most likely has some permanent brain damage. He had memory lapses which could not be explained in any other way. Occasionally he'd completely forget a concept he had mastered one or two days earlier.

JENNY'S STORY

Jenny's travels twist and turn, drift, reverse, and eventually grind to a stop. She describes the fragility of a "cure" and how easily one can veer off the beaten track and plunge back into the abyss of drug usage. Jenny, nearly eighteen, is a nondescript brownhaired white girl who would barely be noticed in the mall. Her weight is proportionate to her height but she has the look of someone who has not bothered to do anything that would tone her musculature.

Her arms and legs have an exaggerated thinness and her slight tummy protrusion looks out of place on someone so young.

Her facial expression is perpetually tense, revealing her inner turmoil. Some days she is unable to concentrate and becomes easily frustrated. However, she completes most of her classroom assignments easily. She should be able to pass the GED test.

Jenny was an ideal drug recruit: unobtrusive appearance, very articulate, and above average in intelligence. Girls such as Jenny are easy individuals to initiate into the drug business. Girls are coveted because they can easily approach strangers in a non-threatening manner and are more readily embraced by their largely male customers.

Sex, usually part of the total arrangement, is not the determining factor in the business relationship. The controlling factor in drug dealing is similar to a legitimate business. Everything is predicated on money. Generally, Jenny's share covers only the expenses of her own habits, little else. Drugs and alcohol are consumed by day; at night Jenny is out selling. CHARGES: under influence controlled substance, possession controlled substance, resisting police officer, curfew

JENNY: ESSAY #16

"In December I was heavily into crystal meth (crystallized methamphetamine). It is one of the easiest drugs to sell and my drug of choice. It caused me to live a very risky life. I could have been dead at the end of each day! I would routinely go for up to two weeks with only about one half-hour of rest to keep me going. I don't know how I escaped getting caught all that time. No legal action was ever taken against me.

"I was out on the streets selling and never went home. The only time I got to see my parents was when I was finally picked up by the police and dropped off at a drug clinic. They called and told them to come take care of me.

"My mom had to be put on Prozac. Even though we didn't have a normal life together they were worried about me. In fact they love me so much they had me kidnaped from that clinic and taken to a facility in another state. I was locked up and not allowed to leave.

"That is where I started what I call real treatment. I stayed locked up for about a month until I dried out (purged drugs from system) and could be transferred to a less restrictive facility. During that time my relationship with Mom and Dad went from not having one to becoming closest friends. I had never felt more proud and happy to be with them.

"I stayed for about four and one half months and during this time my parents and I went to seminars together. They were designed to help us get to know and understand one another better. In addition to the seminars they came down just to visit and that really made it great.

"When I was released and sent home my parents enrolled me in adult education classes and I did great, getting A's in my classes. I was so content staying home and doing good!

"In August when we got out of summer school I decided to spend the night at my friend LuLu's house. We decided it was time to go out and have some fun. Somehow I got left at the party. I got left and then got raped!

"I felt my life was pointless and all I worked for was dumb. I had gone eight months completely sober! That night was the end. Afterward I got high on drugs and booze! Since then I've never been home and never been without a beer in my hand.

"I dealt by running and drinking and that's what I'm in here for; running away and taking up all my bad habits. Today is my court date and they plan to start family counseling for my dependency and my rape. I pray I can bring back my family I love so much and make amends for all the things I regret in my life. Wish me luck!"

COMMENTARY

Many things simply do not add up. How could a loving family neglect Jenny, allowing her to run the streets dealing and consuming drugs? They should have involved the police if they could not intervene themselves.

For Jenny to say that her parents "kidnaped" her is a strange statement. Parents have the right to place their children in treatment centers of their choice. If the courts had severed their parental rights, Jenny should have been assigned a social worker and placed in an appropriate living environment.

Jenny, unable to look directly at anyone, was very closed about certain aspects of her life. I wish I could have talked with her about the party she attended. Why would she deliberately put herself in harm's way? How could her best friend LuLu drive off without checking on her?

Jenny constantly talked about how she felt deeply ashamed of what she had done with her life. Very intelligent, engaging when motivated, and charming in many ways, I hope she can put that shame aside and reassemble her shattered life. Her rape hovered over her life like a black cloud, never completely eradicated from her thoughts. And her deep-seated fear of the grip that drugs have over her weighs heavily on her mind. Intensive counseling and strong support from loved ones can frequently overcome nearly insurmountable handicaps. Jenny is a fighter with an innate capacity to prevail over protracted odds.

CENTER FOR WOMEN POLICY STUDIES

It is essential Jenny receive appropriate, girl-focused guidance, to bolster her resistance to the anger and frustration that consumes her at this time. The Center for Women Policy Studies, founded in 1972, a national, nonprofit, multiethnic and multicultural feminist institution issued a report, fall 1997, urging more research, policy, and programs focusing on girls and violence. "As the Center's report shows, policy makers and researchers have virtually ignored the dramatic increase in the involvement of girls in violent crime and the connection to their own victimization," said Center President Leslie R. Wolfe.

"In 1994, nearly five million women age 12 and older were victims of violent crime, including rape, aggravated assault, robbery and homicide. There was one assault for every 29 women, one rape for every 270 women, one robbery for every 240 women, and one homicide for every 23,000 women, according to the Justice Department" (HandsNet:HN1699, 11-17-97). Girls like Jenny are increasingly responding to the violence they have experienced by fighting back with violence, frequently with knives, guns, and other weapons. The Center for Women Policy Studies convened a summit in late 1997 launching a national effort, focused on the needs of these girls.

CHRISSY'S STORY

A cursory look at Chrissy's home environment gives the impression that all is well. Raised in a nice home in a lower-middle-class neighborhood, Chrissy has never been deprived of adequate food, clothes, or spending money. She describes her parents as being very supportive, loves her brothers and sister, and describes their early years in very positive terms. All the children said they had a decent relationship with their parents.

But all four siblings developed a severe drug addiction, and in the process compiled lengthy juvenile records with the courts. Tragically some family units fail to appropriately integrate healthily into society. This dysfunctional family needed complex repair which, unfortunately, they did not pursue when desperately needed. What appeared to be a two parent family was actually two parents living entirely separate lives. They had very minimal communication between themselves and even less between them and their children.

Chrissy, an average teen, has reasonable classroom skills and enjoys school. Her goal is to get her GED immediately upon her release. Chrissy inherited her Italian father's ruddy complexion with light brown hair cascading to her waist. Well proportioned at five foot, four inches she walked with a little bounce that indicated a girl fairly happy with herself. Chrissy rarely had a problem with other students and got on very well with staff.

Her parents felt they had lost the battle with the streets and, according to Chrissy, had virtually given up on their entire family. They talked about shipping her out to relatives but vacillated, aware that drugs were everywhere.

Chrissy and her parents eventually decided on Utah where one of her father's close friends lived. Chrissy referred to this home as 'rehab.' An extremely active movement there called Straight Edge has members who swore off drugs, drinking, smoking, and casual sex. The <u>Las Vegas Review Journal</u> (12-7-97) reported on this movement and listed the common penalties for members or others who felt their wrath: beatings, brawls, and vandalism of personal property. Chrissy felt very intimidated and insecure around this group. Disillusioned, Chrissy's short stay precluded any long term results.

Her lifestyle would get her in trouble wherever she lived, thus her eventual confinement was healthy at this stage of her life. She returned, stayed with her parents very briefly, then moved in with her boyfriend. There her "bad decisions" resulted in her arrest. CHARGES: robbery, deadly weapon-concealed, burglary, battery deadly weapon, destruction private property

CHRISSY: ESSAY #17

"I was born here sixteen and one-half years ago and have lived here nearly my entire life. We always had a nice house and only moved once to get Mom and Dad closer to work. That was over eight years ago and I loved our new neighborhood immediately. School was good and I finished elementary school with straight A's.

"I never figured to do anything but good at my new school which was called a sixth grade center. This is how they integrated the schools and the first thing I didn't like is taking a bus all the way across town. Most of my friends liked it but I was totally turned off and did lousy work in school.

"My parents felt it was just a phase and we all expected that junior high would be much better. I did have a pretty good year in seventh grade and couldn't wait to reward myself with a super, funfilled summer. I can't explain exactly why but when school ended I just started hanging out, drinking and smoking pot, doing speed, and even eating acid. Anything that was available I did!

"My eighth grade year was terrible and I did not last long because I carried a concealed weapon to school and was expelled. I tried the continuation school for expelled kids, didn't hang long and got back heavy into booze, drugs, and alcohol. When I dropped out my folks decided to try home study and of course that didn't work either.

"By this time I am an alcoholic and an addict and me and my parents decide that I need to try rehabilitation of some kind so they send me to Utah where my Dad's friend lives. I cleaned up for a short while, not long, got scared of the weird people (Straight Edgers) around me and made a quick exit for home.

"Back home my two brothers and sister were still getting high and drinking and I fell right in too. I must say in spite of all this my parents were wonderful and tried to stand behind me and give me support. They were very disappointed in my behavior and told me they couldn't condone what I was doing. They were really hurt!

"I felt guilty and decided to just move out and try living with my boyfriend. He was into drugs heavy and me right along with him. I was sixteen and one half and so messed up I let him talk me into robbing this house. Well, the owners came home and surprised us and things really got out of control. I don't want to get into what happened but when they arrested me four days later and took me to juvenile detention it was actually a relief.

"I've been here for the last three months waiting for a permanent placement until I turn eighteen. My parole officer said I would be confined at least that long.

"I have just explained some important events in my life and maybe you can benefit from them. I wonder why they can't stop the drugs that are being pumped into our neighborhoods. They cause a chain reaction which results in killings, shootings, and gang warfare. My life has been downhill since I discovered drugs!"

COMMENTARY

Nearly all of the literature on delinquency indicates that a strong household can overcome the effects of peer pressure. What went wrong in Chrissy's household? The complete breakdown in communication between the parents and children had a debilitating effect. Many of the parents of troubled children feel that providing the basics of food, lodging, and clothes fulfills their obligation. In truth, children who are deprived in those areas often do much better if they have caring and nurturing adults in their lives. Additionally, siblings who are into the drug scene often feed one another's sickness by constantly exposing each other to drugs and the people who supply them.

BIOCHEMICAL CONSEQUENCES

The Society for Neuroscience, which met in New Orleans on Oct. 27, 1997 revealed for the first time the biochemical consequences of parental neglect on the development of the brain. Harvard University, led by medical school scientist Mary Carlson studied Romanian infants raised in orphanages and reported "that when lacking the attention and stimulation typical of family life, the 2-to-3-year-old children developed abnormally high and lasting levels of the stress hormone cortisol which can have serious long-range effects on learning and memory" (L.A.Times, 10-28-97). Interestingly, the same study revealed that children left in subpar day-care centers had abnormally high levels of stress hormones on week days but tested normal on weekends when the children were back in the home environment.

At the same meeting, the Society presented new animal research data revealing that without proper nurturing the neurons in the brains of infants simply begin to die at an alarming rate. "What we found shocked us," said psychologist Mark Smith at the DuPont Merck Research Labs in Wilmington, Del., who analyzed the effects of maternal deprivation in the laboratory animals. "Maternal separation caused these cells in the brain to die. The effects of maternal deprivation may be much more profound than we had imagined. Does this have implications for humans? Frankly, I hope not, but I suspect there may be." We have known for some time that early childhood deprival of parental sustenance causes long-term behavioral problems and impedes the learning ability of the child.

RAUL'S STORY

Raul, nearly eighteen, never refers to his drug habit in his essay. He blames the lack of 'acknowledgment' from his father for his problems, and feels the murder of his older, role model brother was the impetus for his failure to care what happens to anyone, including himself. He admits to being devious and finds living the 'thug' life natural.

As a youngster, Raul was never forced to face responsibility for his actions. He learned early in life that you could play the system and he became very effective at doing that. He knew exactly how far he could push people--the judge, probation officer, teacher, school policeman, et al--and still avoid confinement. Since Raul did not receive swift and certain punishment for his previous indiscretions, intervention at this stage has been largely ineffective. Juvenile courts deal with truancies, curfew violations, drug use, and even robbery in the initial stages as if they really aren't that consequential. In light of such leniency, many youths are stunned when the gavel finally comes down and they have to deal with serious repercussions for their actions.

Law enforcement in Boston, Massachusetts decided to try to change that. They had a system similar to cities across the nation where "cops don't talk with probation officers and want nothing to do with social workers; nobody wants to work with the fed" (U.S.News & World Report, 1-5-98). These systems fail to carry out punishment promptly and let criminal matters languish for extensive time periods. In their crackdown they tightened goals, told young gang members what the rules were, cooperated with all agencies and made certain enforcement was "swift and certain." Murder is at a 36 year low and among crime-prone 14-to-24 year olds, plunged 65 percent.

Raul would have benefited from that type of intervention during his formative years. A very dark-skinned Hispanic youth Raul, notably physical, likes pumping weights, and eschews sports of all kinds. His six-foot well-proportioned frame boasts layers of muscle in his arms and a "washboard" stomach. His handsome face projects an ironic expression that seems to say, "I'm putting you on." Seldom without a smile, he appears not to have the heavy heart he describes in the essay.

Truancies, curfew violations, drug use, and robbery are prominent in his file. Since the age of eleven he has been a familiar figure in juvenile detention. His escalation into very serious criminal activity doesn't seem to faze him; much as if he's oblivious to its seriousness. CHARGES: under influence unknown substance, possession controlled substance, possession firearm, display weapon, burglary w/deadly weapon, conspiracy commit robbery w/deadly weapon

RAUL: ESSAY #18

"Hi, my name is Raul and I was born right here on a beautiful spring day. I don't remember much about growing up except we moved from neighborhood to neighborhood all around this city. I didn't mind because we had a large family, four brothers and three sisters, and we all stuck up for one another. It was a good family but my father never gave me the acknowledgment I needed. I never got the attention my brothers got so I was the one who would lash out and get attention negatively.

"I decided that if he wouldn't pay me the attention I deserved I would just live the thug life. It was something I didn't have to work at because it was coming naturally to me. The longer I did it the more devious I was becoming.

"My oldest brother was locked up at fifteen and spent several years in prison. I never got a chance to spend much time with him but he was big in my life and it really took a toll on me when he got murdered. The sixteenth day out of prison he was "wasted" (killed). He was the only role model I had because my dad was in and out and didn't pay much attention to me.

"When Isaac got murdered that triggered something in me and it started a wilder lifestyle than ever. My life was action packed with drama and pain, just like the movies. Shootings and brawls were daily things. I guess there was just no way I could get over the death of Isaac.

"I remember watching the news and seeing my mother cry. This really hurt me. It gave me this feeling in my heart that I shouldn't care about what happens with anyone including myself. I know that Isaac is never going to return. I'm trying to do positive things with my life but the passing of my role model will always effect me."

COMMENTARY

Raul, a typical youngster whose file of minor violations started at a very young age, knew that committing crimes rarely resulted in anything more than a reprimand. His probation officer had a huge caseload and spent more time with major offenders, so he rarely harried Raul. This is one major failure of the juvenile process. The younger offenders are those most likely to respond to supervision but ironically receive the least attention.

Close to 18, he has some very serious charges, and his nonchalant attitude about the seriousness of his crimes is startling. His prognosis? Certification as an adult and an aimless trek through the adult judicial (criminal) system. He did not heed much from the example of his "role model" brother and is choosing the same dismal path for himself. In his mind, there is an apparent glamorization of the whole prison process. He is not alone in this attitude. Such teens never connect with the bleak and sterile conditions life in prison forces you to endure.

Raul didn't respond to counseling and considered it akin to a threat if you pointed out the things that would happen to him if he were not to change. Psychologist Christopher N. Bacorn of Texas feels that boys like Raul really can't make use of professional counseling. "What a boy can use, and all too often doesn't have, is the fellowship of men--at least one man who pays attention to him, who spends time with him, who admires him. A boy needs a man he can look up to. What he doesn't need is a shrink" (Newsweek, My Turn, 12-7-92). Bacorn describes the things that absent fathers are doing: drinking in taverns, playing pool with other men, golf, tennis, bowling, fishing, working extra jobs, or doing mundane chores at home. "In short, they are everywhere, except in the company of their children." His message was that when boys lack a sense of how a man should behave they model their behavior on someone out there on the street corner or in this case an inappropriate sibling in the home.

Many of the girls who wind up in juvenile detention lack supervision at home, are abused, and face exposure to drugs and other illegal activities at a young age. An alarming number--estimated as high as 70 percent of girls in juvenile facilities--are abused either sexually, emotionally, or physically in their own home. This figure is shocking enough but many of the juvenile court personnel I talked with felt the percentage was actually much higher.

The federal government estimates that 23 to 34 percent of young women in the general population have been sexually abused. Intake studies of girls in the juvenile justice system show that 50 to 70 percent are sexually, physically, or emotionally abused--with the high end on sexual. (L.A.Times, 7-9-96)

Child abuse and neglect in California have risen sharply over the past decade, which is reflected in states throughout the country.

Between 1985 and 1994 the number of reported abuse cases jumped 133 percent according to the California Legislative Analyst's office. The state's assembly judiciary committee released statistics confirming that the drug epidemic is responsible for 70 to 90 percent of all abuse resulting in a child being removed from the home (1995).

Providing adequate care for girls is extremely difficult. There are simply not enough facilities designed to provide alternative living space. Placed in inappropriate settings, these girls run away. FBI figures for 1996 show that 57 percent of juvenile runaways are females. A 1994 study by the American Correctional Association found sexually abused girls to be at greater risk of engaging in prostitution than other runaways. Incredibly, these runaways are often returned to the very environment that engendered the abuse or neglect.

MARY'S STORY

Mary is a striking example of this. She never had a genuine chance in life because of the appalling circumstances in which she was forced to live. A frail 17-year-old with the desperate look of someone badly needing to be nurtured, she is very meticulous about everything she does. Her hair is always done in a particular style, her clothes always look freshly ironed, and her books and papers are all carefully arranged on her desk. She spends inordinate amounts of time checking and rechecking her work. She re-wrote the following essay several times before she felt it reflected exactly the way she wanted to portray her life.

Ironically, the end of her story is rather vague. I suspect she found the details too painful to recall and commit to her essay. CHARGES: traffic warrant, evading police officer, reckless driving, false information, curfew, no drivers license, possession/use controlled substance

MARY: ESSAY #19

"I was born in 1979 to my mother, Imelda, who was only fifteen years old. My mother was young and not so ready to be a mother to such a little one who needed her most. She tried to carry out a mother's job to the best of her knowledge, but just couldn't do it. So when I was four years old I moved in with my grandma.

"Grandma's house wasn't the best either. My grandma was a very caring person and allowed everyone into her home. She made me believe you could save the whole world. My uncles were addicts and lived off my grandma for everything she had to offer. My uncles would go on drug runs with money they had stolen from her. They were heartless. During this time I tried to stay out of everyone's way because I was considerate of my grandma who had her hands full and I didn't want to add to her burden.

"I was eleven years old when I discovered alcohol, cigarettes, and boys. I decided to try staying away from home. I just couldn't stand being there all the time. I ran around doing whatever I wanted. I stole money to give to my friends or to buy things I wanted.

"When I was twelve my grandma died and that must have alerted the authorities that they had to do something with me. I was then forced to live with my mom and my father(?), neither of whom I even knew. That's when it really started. I spent seven days in a mental hospital because they didn't understand why I wouldn't go with my parents.

"It was bad but I lived with my parents and their drugs for about a year and a half. In between this time I had made my own friends and started my own drug habit. My drugs got me locked up for six months in this little town up north.

"When I got out of the Adolescent Drug Center up there I had no control...just kept doing more and more drugs. My father moved me around to get me away from my friends, but every place we went I still carried it out.

"Nobody would leave me alone so I started running away. They would catch me and put me on probation and I would just run again. They didn't have any place to keep me so they finally court ordered me to move down here with my father's mother.

"I thought I was pregnant at the time and refused to come down here. Bill, my boyfriend, begged me to stay and I felt I had to do that for my baby's father. We became runaways and eventually were caught. The court order was executed and now I am here awaiting the court's placement."

COMMENTARY

Mary had a bleak outlook from birth, moving from foster home to foster home during those periods when Protective Services removed her from her mother's care. During this time, unable to talk to anyone about the worst aspects of her life, she suffered in silence. Though reluctant and with obvious reservations, the state eventually placed her with the grandmother. Apparently good hearted and well-meaning, this grandmother was totally inappropriate for a desperate young girl.

She had vague recollections, from a very early age, of her mother's bouts with intoxication. Mary described these bouts as being a time when "everything stood still." No food, no television, nothing but her mother and an acquaintance doing drugs and communicating in this drunken state. Both totally ignored Mary.

She remembered being hungry and cold during her early years with her mother. With Grandma, the depravity was entirely different. That household also exposed her to drugs, as well as "things" that Mary wished she'd never seen. When asked why she ran away, she'd respond: "It was terrible." Mary has felt powerless her entire life. Resigned now to another placement, she professes this will last only until her eighteenth birthday.

She wants to break the cycle, desperate to prove she can take care of herself, get a good job, and live a good life. And one day be a good mother.

Society profoundly underestimates and underreacts to the physical, emotional, and sexual abuse young children endure daily throughout this country. Juvenile drug abuse is directly related to the neglect and abuse experienced in the home. The U.S Office for Substance Abuse Prevention (OSAP) identifies several "familial factors associated with alcohol and other drug (AOD) use or addiction and dependency among children and youth:]Susceptibility to dependence by virtue of being a member of a family in which alcohol dependence or drug addiction spans one or more generations]Being a member of a family where parents hold favorable attitudes toward AOD use or in which parents themselves, model use of alcohol or other drugs]Being reared by parents whose discipline is slack, inconsistent, or authoritarian or without maternal involvement, perceived warmth, or closeness" (U.S. OSAP Prevention Monograph-8, 1991). Drugs are the decay that we must successfully address in both public and private institutions. Studies statistically show that underlying most of our basic problems in the juvenile sector is the overwhelming growth in illicit drug use.

Florida Republican Representative Bill McCollum, chairman of the House Judiciary subcommittee on crime, is the sponsor of the Juvenile Crime Control Act of 1997. A major part of the bill would give juvenile judges the authority to fine or otherwise sanction parents for not following court orders designed to force them to act responsibly in overseeing a child's behavior. This is desperately needed. Unless we somehow force the people who are having babies to accept the responsibility for their well-being we will continue to witness the tragedies described in this book. Unfortunately the courts will have to play an increasing role if this is to be accomplished. "It will not be exclusively through the official system. It will require the involvement of friends, family and neighbors willing to become involved, willing to make a call, willing to offer support. We need school programs that emphasize alternatives to getting pregnant and keeping babies that are unwanted...there are a lot of families that would want to adopt the child," says Deanne Tilton, executive director of the Los Angeles County Inter-Agency Council on Child Abuse and Neglect (L.A.Times, 3-28-96).

Drug use triggers the abuse and neglect that has to be addressed if these babies are to survive and develop compos mentis! This is a complex problem that will not be easily solved. The students featured in these essays who have babies easily are in the majority. Every new study indicates these numbers are increasing. Their babies cry out to us. We must make crucial decisions and be ready to back these decisions with action. What chance do they have otherwise?

Chapter 5

PROSTITUTION
Only Recourse For Troubled Females

Of all the juvenile delinquents, girls who enter the strange, dangerous world of prostitution are the heaviest risk takers. What is the profile of the teenager (or sometimes pre-teen) who enters this nightmare lifestyle, one ruled by unprincipled pimps who are governed by greed? In small towns, pimps can easily spot girls on "the prowl" because there are only a few places where they hang out, and they tend to be more naive than girls from the cities.

Most girls have already experienced various delinquency-related problems, including drug use. Their parents or guardians view them as out of control teens with no interest in school. At home, these teens had defiant attitudes; arguments with parents which included physical confrontations. They'd flaunt the rules and have contempt for authority.

The young girls with whom I worked, described their pimps as racially mixed males from poor backgrounds. All pimps had several things in common: They drove big expensive cars (used for turning "tricks"[*] on the road), possessed a variety of drugs, were glib talkers, and knew exactly how to entice vulnerable young girls into their cars for recruitment. From that point they totally controlled the life of these girls.

How could these teens evolve from total defiance of authority and being out of control to becoming totally subservient to their pimps? Drugs play a key initial role in such control. Physical intimidation is another major factor with scars on many girls as living proof. (One young girl has the imprint of a hot iron on her stomach, which she will have for the rest of her life!)

---

[*] "Trick" is a term used for any sex act performed for money.

At the outset, this prostitution "trip" seems like a big party, with their craving for drugs easily satisfied. But soon their "work" begins--and it is grueling. The girls claim they use protection, and have a regular clientele of relatively safe customers; in reality however, they must be available to anyone willing to pay for their "services." If they refuse customers and return to their pimp with too little money, they face physical abuse and withholding of drugs.*

Girls receive a nominal amount for a fast-food meal, makeup and hair salons, and a new street outfit. They never see any money beyond this.

Ironically, these girls choose to languish in confinement, rather than testify in court against their pimp. I've watched them have their release delayed by weeks because of strong feelings for their pimp. Is it loyalty or fear? Clearly, it seems evident they have been brainwashed to believe they must protect this person. While this defies logic, it is repeated ad nauseam, and unfortunately works for the pimp.

PROSTITUTION ENIGMA

An emerging part of the prostitution enigma is the exploitation of immigrants. Thailand is particularly fertile grounds for these "recruiters" because of low educational levels, extreme poverty, and a cultural tradition which holds females in low esteem and vulnerable. In his L.A.Times article, "Easy Prey: Exploiting Immigrants," Don Lee describes this exploitation. "The Buddhist notion of fatalism and an abiding sense of obligation in Thailand's rigid hierarchical society combine to make uneducated Thais perfect victims--silent and resigned to their lot" (1/13/97).

Mr. Lee quotes Assistant D.A. David Lanine, who points out how women are "duped into thinking they will be living the American dream in essence, only to find that they are stuck in a life of prostitution until they can pay off their debts." These

---

* All prostitution money is handled totally by the pimps.

debts often exceed thousands of dollars leaving these girls controlled by smugglers for years. Immigration officials estimate that these young girls are being smuggled into the West Coast at a rate of 100 per month.

SATANIC CONNECTION

Many of the students in detention, male and female, practiced different forms of Satanic worship. A pimp often will use this fascination with Satanic principles as a recruiting device if he senses interest in a potential proselyte. The case of Danny Scherts, arrested by the FBI under the Mann Act--AKA the White Slave Traffic Law--on suspicion of transporting a teenager across state lines for prostitution illustrates this. Staff writer Davan Maharaj described the following scenario: "Before their departure, Schertz gave R.D.E. (girl's identity in court documents) a "slave bracelet" and pentagram, a five-pointed star signifying that R.D.E. was his property" (L.A. Times, 12-27-95). FBI agent Leonardo D. Floyd said Schertz used the citizen's band radio in his van to solicit truck driver customers at designated truck stops.

LOREN"S STORY

The escort and exotic-dancer business has a strong link to prostitution. One of my students was a dancer, loved her work and could not wait to get back to her "profession." She was unusual because she talked about the home she'd purchased, her infatuation with Las Vegas, and the fact that she hated to travel because of a deep-seated fear of flying. She did not fit the profile of the stereotypical underage prostitute. There were many questions I did not get to ask her. She was nearly eighteen and never reappeared in detention.

Loren became involved in prostitution when a man she met sensed her vulnerability and recruited her. Beautiful, intelligent, and articulate, Loren is an extreme risk taker. She does whatever is deemed appropriate for the moment. Although she understands her vulnerability, she is fueled by a restless imagination, aware that it can lead her deeper into this morass.

Loren will get money at any cost, heedless of the consequences. She has multiple criminal charges in her file. She admitted to a host of illegal activities that led to her incarceration. She views these activities as degrading and regrets they could bring shame to her family (with whom she has no contact), yet fears that doing the right thing would be far too confining. CHARGES: solicitation for prostitution, false information, material witness, out of jurisdiction

LOREN: ESSAY #20

"Born seventeen years ago to Michelle and James, my parents, I was not a particularly healthy baby due to colic and continuous ear infections. Even with minor health problems I still had a very happy and fulfilling first five years of my life. During that period I spent all the time I could with my mother and my father.

"Suddenly everything changed! My mother found out she was pregnant with my little sister and decided she needed a job. All of the individual attention I had previously received from my mother vanished. However, I managed to attend elementary school and be successful regardless of all the changes at home.

"In second grade I took an interest in figure skating and became very involved. I continued to skate all the way up through the seventh grade as it became a very important, dedicated part of my life.

"In the seventh grade my long-time coaches retired and no one else in town was qualified to teach me. So, after much thought was put into the decision, there was nothing to do but quit.

"I then had to find myself again. Middle school was uncomfortable for me as it was for most of the young people at the school. High school was a world of difference and I began to discover and become very fond of the woman I was becoming.

"I somehow acquired a shoplifting problem. When I got caught for the third time I was put on six month probation and because of the consequences facing me I couldn't chance doing it anymore.

So I started embezzling money from my jobs!

"In June I had just gotten fired from my last job when I met an individual who was immediately aware of my vulnerable situation. He took advantage of it by manipulating me into selling my body to give him an income.

"I've violated my parole three times since then, all with this individual. Now I am waiting because they are making me testify against him.

"Hopefully I can go on with my life in a more positive way. I would like to become the successful woman I have the potential to be!"

COMMENTARY

Little was known about Loren's background. She had lost all contact with her parents, and did not talk about family except to hold them responsible for the pressures that overwhelmed her life. She felt no need to allow them along on her "journey" yet she felt guilty for how she had polluted her life and caused them anguish.

Aware of her need for counseling, she felt anxious to break emotional ground, in search of answers. Seduced by money, her nemesis, she desperately needed help to grasp the reality of life free of crime. For her to stop this cycle of arrests and escalating crime would require intense and ongoing therapy. Hopefully, getting this help will be a condition of her release; pre-arranged so that she will not be able to dismiss it as unimportant or unaffordable. There are programs within the community which are available to her, but they require a dedication Loren doesn't always exhibit. There are even a few homes throughout the nation, such as Genesis House in Chicago, which try to "restructure the personality" of these young women and help them make the slow journey into the mainstream.

CASSANDRA'S STORY:

Cassandra (Cass to her friends in confinement) belonged to a group of prostitutes who traveled with Andre, a pimp, to many West Coast cities. Described as "very slick" by Cass, she felt strongly that Andre was "too smart" to ever become entangled with the courts.

A big girl with a good sense of humor, Cass had a penchant for off-the-wall remarks. She treated everything irreverently, feeling everyone took life too seriously. She refused to be daunted by such feelings. She had a simple, basic approach to life: She wanted things her way. Though listed as Caucasian on the booking sheet, Cass has an ethnically complex skin type with a darker tone that contrasts with her naturally blondish hair. When angered she'd warn: "Don't get this 'Injun' mad." If you traced her bloodline, she probably was partially Native-American. Cass used this unique attractiveness to her advantage.

Although Cass refers to her mother and father in her essay, they were noticeably uninvolved in her juvenile detention problems. Reared in the tradition of obedience and deference to her father, she tired of his dictatorial ways at a very young age. Her mother played an undefined role in her younger years, and did not get involved with the issues that would ultimately dominate Cass's life. CHARGES: Out of jurisdiction runaway (OJ), solicitation for prostitution-two charges, obstruction public police officer, curfew

CASS: ESSAY #21

"My life is not all that good. I can't remember much about my early life until I was five years old and moved to Alabama. That's when it all started.

"I hated school and eventually just stopped going. I told my parents it was the school system where we lived in this little town. It was easy to move around down there so we moved to a bigger town and I went to a different school. But I still didn't go to school! By this time two years had passed. I stopped going to school so my parents tried, without success, to do home school. Nothing was working and my dad asked me if I would try regular school again. I said yes, went back to school, got into all kinds of trouble and again quit going.

"I started having trouble with the law right after that because of truancy and other things I was doing. They pulled me into court and I was put on probation for one year. I got in trouble again for not going to school but they didn't lock me up, they put me on a monitor for six months. David, my probation officer, waited until my six months were up on the monitor and came to my house to cut it off. After they cut off the monitor they took me down and locked me up on some more bullshit charges!

"This was in February two years ago and I sat in there for two months before they committed me. Once I got to court they committed me for six months of incarceration. I finally got out the following September. I never got in trouble while in confinement but I was STILL placed on six months probation once I got out. In two months I turned seventeen and was viewed as an adult in that state.

"They really scared the crap out of me when they said if I got into any more trouble I was going to the adult jail. I was broke and depressed and they convinced me I did not want any part of that scene.

"One day I was driving and got a ticket. Then I got a few more. I went and put them on a payment plan, never paid, and got locked up just like they said I would. Same thing happened again and the cops began making it extremely uncomfortable for me there.

"I met this guy at the end of the summer. A pimp. He went to Miami with three other girls, called me and said he'd send money for a plane ticket. I took a plane down there and started walking the streets. Vice started messing with all of us so we picked out some other places and ended up here on Halloween.

"Me and Andre got into a fight, mostly just words, and I told him I wanted to go home on the plane. I made reservations but he never came up with the plane ticket so I called my mom and told her I wanted to come home but nothing happened. That night I was back out on the tracks with the other girls. And now I'm here!

"I have learned something since I've been here. I have a

weak mind. I need to work on that! When I get out on the fourteenth of this month I'm going home to my mom if she wants me."

COMMENTARY

What Cass describes as a "weak mind" may more accurately describe her need for instant gratification, heedless of the consequences. Extremely impulsive, she did not take direction well, and enjoyed the cat-and-mouse games she played on the streets with law enforcement. To survive in the "world's oldest profession", you need some life sustaining fear but Cass had none. She had to be described as exceptional, when even her pimp could not control her.

Cass responded to school only on her terms. She worked diligently on her writing skills but would not touch mathematics, even though she needed to improve those skills if she hoped to pass the GED test. It will be a formidable task for Cass and her mother putting the pieces of their lives back together. There is such a small separation between success and failure, but hopefully they can fight through the stunning number of obstacles and reconstruct this bewitching young lady's future.

SUZ'S STORY:

Suz targets family divorce as the point where life suddenly started a downward spiral. Indicators in her story point to an unstable existence during most of her younger years. These years focused on her skating. When she quit, it seemed to sap the stability from her life. (The importance of athletic involvement and other organized activities for youngsters needs to be more highly emphasized, and encouraged.)

Suz felt no shame about being a prostitute, but felt she had also failed at that. She lasted only one night in this new setting and felt terrible that her arrest would ultimately end with the incarceration of her pimp. She knew her testimony would have to eventually come and that delays were futile. She expressed concern for her safety and that of her family. Convinced that her pimp would retaliate violently, she added that she really couldn't blame him for that!

Her scowl highlighted her attractive, yet startling face. She looked like a young waif with a permanent pout. Her smile, an oddly embarrassed one, caused her to turn away quickly, only to return with a blank stare. Her pale complexion, almost ghost-like, never changed despite time spent outside under the blazing desert sun. CHARGES: solicitation for prostitution, false ID, material witness, loitering for prostitution, curfew

SUZ: ESSAY #22

"When I was a child my life was simple. I started skating, my first obsession, at three years old. I went to school on the base until fourth grade and then we moved.

"I then switched to another elementary school and finished up sixth grade there. That is when I started middle school and also when the trouble started. I had to stop skating, absolutely my favorite interest, when my father left my mother. We couldn't afford lessons any more, and at that point my life started to go downhill. I stayed at that school for about three months until Mom pulled me out and put me into a school closer to her work. I stayed there for three years doing pretty good except my grades were just fair and I was truant a lot.

"My ninth grade I started a new high school and did just terrible. I then started moving schools a lot, making three changes in just one year. Nothing seemed to work for me!

"During this same year my mother met this guy named Lee and moved in with him causing me another school change. He owned a hardware store and made great money. Sadly, we never got along.

I went to that high school for half of tenth grade and simply dropped out. My mother then kicked me out and I went to live with my grandma.

"When I moved into that neighborhood there was nothing to do but hang out. That is when I met LeRoy. I became a prostitute and did pretty well for about one year. Then LeRoy said there was easy money and good times on the road so we hopped in his Mercedes and eventually ended up here. I'm so dumb I only lasted one day and got busted (arrested) for soliciting.

"I've been here about a month and feel I have done pretty good in school and could probably pass my test when I get out. I have to testify before they will let me out and that is scary. I hope nothing happens to me or my family. That pretty much sums up my life."

COMMENTARY

Most of Suz's problems centered around status offenses and nonviolent activity such as prostitution. F.B.I. statistics (1994) on incarcerated girls in the U.S.A. indicate nearly three-fourths had nonviolent or status offense charges. For Suz these status offenses included truancy, violating curfew, incorrigibility, and being a runaway. These are typical juvenile crimes and she will not have to deal with them when she turns eighteen. However, her caseworker considered the problems associated with her pimp extremely serious. LeRoy, described as violent and dangerous, had a record of retaliation when someone "rolled over" (testified against) on him. Caseworkers wouldn't speculate on prison time he might serve, but my guess is less than five years. Pimps generally serve only about one third of their sentence, rarely experience a transformation while in prison, and often have long memories.

Prosecutors must deal more effectively with pimps! An important step is to diligently litigate statutory rape cases. Many state laws deal specifically with prostitution, but not specifically with underage prostitution. In most states, sex with a minor under the age of fourteen is considered child abuse. At age fourteen and older it is deemed unlawful sex with a minor, or statutory rape. In both situations it doesn't matter if the sex is consensual.

BAUNIA'S STORY:

Baunia, on the streets since age twelve, has two children

who travel around the country with her. She is one of the more opinionated persons I have ever talked with about juvenile justice. She feels there is no "justice" and will be happy when she turns eighteen and is free of the chains that court "protection" offers her.

A tense person, she appears nervous and unsure of herself much of the time. She refuses to discuss the scars on her arms and legs. Her black hair is permanently in corn rows, and her dark brown eyes show flashes of fire when angered. This attractive black girl wanted her "space", giving very menacing looks if invaded.

Sadly there is little chance that Baunia will change her behavior. She enjoys her travels which she describes as being in style and with class. Typically, prostitutes move from city to city so they aren't easily recognized by vice officers. Those who stay in one location become easy targets and are routinely arrested in periodic "sweeps" of known areas of prostitution. The younger girls like Bueania are afforded the luxury of travel until their beauty fades and the pimp recruits a younger replacement. CHARGES: minor in casino, material witness, OJ/runaway

BAUNIA: ESSAY #23

"My name is Baunia and I was born in Ohio. At the time I was born my mom and dad lived in a two story brick home with seven bedrooms. I remember it as being so nice! We lived there until my mother left us and we could no longer afford it.

NOTE: The seven bedroom home described above was part of the estate her father helped maintain as a gardener/landscaper.

"It was then just me and my Pops. I had to go to work with him everyday. He was a landscaper and it was enjoyable really. When I turned five he put me in an early education class because he wanted me to do well in school. At six I went to a Christian school and stayed until I finished fifth grade.

"Pops wasn't doing all that well at work and said it was time for me to go to public school. I went for all of one week and then started to live in the streets. I was just twelve.

"Now I'm seventeen and locked up in this place. I've been to every major city and have been living quite well. I love to travel and hope to spend the rest of my life traveling around the world.

"I have no serious charges against me. I'm being held as a material witness with a $20,000 bond. But I should leave soon.

In order for me to leave I have to testify, along with two other girls who were with me. None of us want to testify but we have no choice. That is the way the system works and we have no control over it, according to our lawyer.

"If we don't cooperate we will be held on contempt of court charges. I don't want that because I wouldn't be able to go back to Ohio with my kids. So the only thing to do is testify. Then I can leave."

COMMENTARY

In her appearance and dialogue, Beaunia is far from the stereo-typical prostitute. One might even imagine her as a law student. Clearly, the major domo in her small circle, her conversations are laced with legal terms. Although she didn't express outright contempt for the juvenile system she continually questioned a legal system that safeguarded her from herself. The status offenses for which she was charged were not criminal. She considered them a slight nuisance.

Juvenile courts were first established in the early 20th century and were based on the paternalistic assumption that adults know what is best for children. In the 1960's "The Supreme Court extended limited civil rights to youngsters accused of criminal behavior. Juvenile court was now clearly adversarial and based in part on due process principles. Children are generally denied two fundamental rights available to adults, the right to a trial by jury and the right to bail, although some states have extended these rights" (<u>Critical Issues in Child Welfare,</u> Gustavsson-Segal[*]). Beaunia's main complaint was that

---

[*] Sage Publications 1994

she was denied these two rights. She contended that if these rights were intact the courts could then concentrate on the real tasks facing them in a more meaningful and comprehensive manner. It seemed like a giant leap, rationalization gone amuck, but we had some interesting discussions on the subject.

CECELIA'S STORY

Many of the girls sent to detention for prostitution view their life a big adventure which they are eager to continue. Fully aware of the risks involved, they have a fatalistic attitude. Cecelia describes herself as a dancer and personal entertainer. She admits to absolutely nothing other than that. Her creed is, "you are born, you grow up, then you die."

A very tall, thin Hispanic girl, Cecelia can change her total appearance merely with different hair styles! Her lovely face looks entirely different each time her style changes. Her figure is superb and complements her overall appearance. Cecelia describes herself as a "trophy."

Like so many other girls, she has been on her own for many years; since age eleven, according to her essay. CHARGES: solicitation for prostitution/three counts, loitering for prostitution, drug paraphernalia

CECELIA: ESSAY #24

"My present lifestyle started when my mom sent me to live with my aunt in Washington after I had just turned eleven. I have never seen my father and I never lived with my mother after I turned eleven. I have been basically making my own way since eleven years of age.

"When I was fourteen they picked me up and sent me back to live with my mother. I moved out almost as soon as I got there and was pregnant at fifteen. I had my baby just after I turned sixteen and decided to move around. Since 1995 my life has been a big, wonderful adventure!

"However, that adventure led me to this dump. I've been in juvenile since October--about six weeks. When I get out I'll be a lot more careful because this is the last time. There is a first time for everything and this is also the last. So, my adventure will never end! Thank you!"

COMMENTARY

It is frightening to even contemplate her "adventure," but it is clear Cecilia feels ready to meet it head on. She talks about networking, presumably with prostitutes, to care for her baby. (Apparently children do not interfere with the 'great adventure' to any large degree.)

She did not talk about a pimp. Other girls knew Cecilia from the streets but she did not mix well with them. She tended to be very secretive about herself and her life. Adamant about her disdain for juvenile detention, she was equally adamant about avoiding incarceration in the future.

It both amazes and alarms those who work with teen prostitutes how little regard they have for their personal safety. Cecilia refused to acknowledge the dangers of prostitution. She feared gender-based laws the most. It seemed apparent that nothing could deter her from living her adventure, and that she'd continue to flout society's 'moral standards'.

Girls, who are more likely to run away from home than boys, survive under the harshest conditions. They rarely hesitate to change their physical surroundings when necessary. According to FBI figures 57 percent of juvenile runaways are females. A 1994 study by the American Correctional Association also found sexually abused girls to be at greater risk than either other runaway girls or runaway boys for engaging in prostitution. (L.A.Times, Jagged Justice, 7/9/96)

The article also quotes Laura Axtell of Associated Marine Institutes (private residential and treatment programs), that abused girls will run from anywhere. "They will run in the middle of the night, with no shoes on, by themselves. They are absolutely so resilient--because they are survivors, survivors of abuse."

KATE'S STORY

Kate is the prototype of a bonafide survivor who feels the need to change environments frequently. Although no apparent history of abuse from her two stepfathers, if you read between the lines their are indicators. She has never seen her biological father and has a very poor relationship with her mother. CHARGES: OJ/Runaway, possession controlled substance, loitering prostitution, soliciting prostitution

KATE: ESSAY #25

"The movie said life was like a box of chocolates. You never know what flavor you're gonna get. Well, I would have to disagree with Gump, the simple-minded character in the movie, and say that life is what you make it (I believe). If you work hard enough, ninety-nine-point-nine percent of the time you're gonna get it.

"In my life I need to pay more attention to that fact. I also should pay more attention to the advice the people who care for me give me. I realize now that I should've been more grateful to their advice than more hateful. It's too late for that now but it's not too late to make changes.

"Me mess of a life, as I call it, started back east in Virginia seventeen years ago at Village Square Hospital. I was raised in Virginia. I have grown up knowing one or two facts about my real father and nothing else. I grew up knowing everything about my first and second stepfathers.

"I first started messing up my life in my junior year of high school. I just decided to leave home and went to another state without my parents permission.

"When I decided to return from my month-long journey they made me immediately withdraw from school. I left my "B" and high "C" grades behind. I decided to get my GED, then get a job in the summer while doing adult education, so I could get my high school diploma also.

"I was doing good and had a wonderful Christmas. After the holidays my mom decided she was tired of me coming in whenever I pleased without calling. So she told me to leave. I had no problem with leaving. So I did!

"I've been gone from my house since that December and really haven't been getting into any trouble. I don't know what happened, but now here I am in some juvenile detention facility all the way across the country. For the first time I'm scared. I think it's time to turn around. Completely!

"I would like to change my name to "Angel" because I am a caring person and I enjoy doing nice things for others. I also like to make people smile. Making others happy helps me to feel better about myself."

COMMENTARY

What an ironic ending to her story! "For the first time I'm scared." Now wanting to change her name to Angel because she enjoys "doing nice things for others." In those revealing words, one can feel her pain and hear her cry for help as she tries to turn her life around. There is also a lot of anger, anger at her mother who seemed to constantly reject her even when things were going fairly well. This has left her feeling confused, rejected and full of suffering. Will her mother finally take a genuine interest in her? There's a deep need for acceptance.

HELENA'S STORY

This story contrasts Kate's essay. When Helena began her studies, she challenged everything I said, or she concluded I said, as I helped her with assignments. She is very bitter about the existing double standard between boys and girls in detention, a theme heard daily from most of the girls, convinced that if she had been a male she'd never have been arrested. Instead she'd be living the life she carved out for herself at the vulnerable age of 14, when she ran away from her adoptive parents.

She is very aggressive, never ducks an argument, and is quick to challenge anyone, going into a physically intimidating posture on the slightest provocation. A tall, athletic African-American she more than holds her own in the coed-volleyball

games played in the quad area. Helena is extremely strong and uses her strength to enhance her seemingly unlimited athletic skills. I had to keep her away from the boys in the class because of the inevitable conflict if they were in close proximity of her.
CHARGES: bench warrant served, petty larceny, false information, runaway, solicitation for prostitution

HELENA: ESSAY #26

"My name is Helena and I was adopted when I was two-and-one-half-years old. I was born in Boise, Idaho and when adopted moved to Las Vegas, Nevada and that is where I lived until running away from home. My childhood life was pretty good until I turned eight. That is when all of the trouble began.

"I was put into an institution called CBS, Children's Behavioral Services. After two months they said I was better and let me go. It didn't really work and I was sent back two more times. After the third time I thought things were going pretty well. For a while that is. When I turned thirteen I started running away from home.

They took me home, put me in school and I would run again.

"Then one day in eighth grade I beat up this girl named Micky. It was a pretty bad fight and I got suspended and told to leave campus. But I wouldn't! I stayed on campus and fought some more so they had to get a truant officer to drive me home.

"I didn't want to go home so I gave the lady the wrong directions. She finally got completely fed up with me and we went back to the school. My mom talked with her, gave her the correct directions, and we headed for my house. I knew the trouble was just beginning for me so on the way home I opened the door and jumped out of the moving car. I went directly to the highway and hitched a ride to the Coast.

"I worked on the streets, sold drugs, and took care of my own self. That was three years ago and they just caught up with me and brought me here as a runaway. I'll be eighteen in two-and-one-half months. Why don't they leave me alone?"

COMMENTARY

A sad story. Helena is a damaged child who must have had very serious childhood problems to warrant placement in CBS. As a former principal, I know it is difficult to place a child in CBS even when the child is obviously in desperate need of treatment.

She will not be regarded as a juvenile when she turns eighteen in less than three months. Obviously a survivor, there is a certain maturity about her, except that she clearly lacks self-awareness. She sees no need to make changes in her life or lifestyle. She lives in the dangerous world of prostitution and drugs and has very few skills for survival in the mainstream society. What decision could her probation officer and the judge make that would aid in healing this young lady and set her on a healthy path?

There are very few reform efforts for these girls, but the trap they seek to escape is one of the most difficult imaginable. The Mary Magdalene Project is one of very few groups in the entire country which assists prostitutes to learn skills for living in society. Jill Leovy writes: "For such women, leaving the streets is not just a matter of willpower. They often cannot tell time, read a calendar or find a number in a telephone book. The nonprofit group bought a 12-unit apartment building [in Van Nuys, California] earlier this year that is now home to Irene and eight other women who are making the slow journey into the mainstream" (L.A.Times, 12-2-96). There is a desperate need for programs like this to be duplicated and expanded throughout our cities. Officer Esther Kunz [LAPD], quoted in the above article, said--"It is so sad after awhile, you arrest them over and over again. You ask, 'What can I do for them?' And there's nothing. No referral. Nothing...it is so hopeless. You start thinking, 'I don't know why I do this.'"

Helena will most likely fall into this rut, adapting to the street mentality that provides her with survival skills in that dangerous world. The Genesis House in Chicago is the only other residential housing for former prostitutes. Those who make the decisions that will impact Helena's future have limited resources in terms of a potential placement. Conversely, would she even consider placement if offered one?

TYPICAL RECRUIT

A Hollywood streetwalker at the tender age of 12, Irene became a heavy drug user and had 23 arrests by her early twenties. She is a typical resident recruited for the program from jail. Most of the girls in my detention program began their odyssey at that approximate young age. Imagine these naive girls entering a car with a complete stranger and leaving home for a far-away destination! Impossible to contemplate how their gullibility sucks them under. When the reality of their plight hits them, they must feel completely vulnerable and trapped. Unfortunately, by that time these girls are easily intimidated. (Pimps have intimidation down to a science!)

AUDREY'S STORY

Audrey looks like a typical wholesome teenager from 'Littletown,' Minnesota. A very light-skinned Caucasian, her personality is a unique mix of intrigue, insights, and humor. She has an opinion on virtually everything but is not seriously into anything that will cause stress in her life. Audrey picks the easiest educational packets and then browses through them doing just the very easiest assignments. Her folder is very thick with half-finished packets. In her opinion there should be more computer preparation that doesn't require the laborious task of doing everything by hand. She's not even sure a GED is going to be beneficial in her eventual career choice. At this point in her life an OJT (on the job training) track is the one she will pursue. Audrey's procrastination consumes her waking hours and prevents the progress she could easily make toward acquiring the necessary skills she'll need in life.

AUDREY: ESSAY #27

"Early one fall morning my mother was awakened from her

sleep with a strange pain in her stomach. It was me and she says that pain has never gone away. A little girl with brown curly hair and big brown eyes arrived that day amid a swirling snow storm in upper Minnesota. We lived there until I was seven years old and then my mother and I moved to Northern California until I was twelve years old. That is when my troubles started.

"I would get into trouble and me and my mother would sit and argue, frequently far into the night. The longer we argued the more she drank and the crazier our conversations became. I began discreetly sipping along and developed a strong liking for alcohol. Then drugs surfaced in my life and with drugs the association with others who were also into it.

"I got arrested many times for shoplifting, stealing, and runaway. Nearly all of those charges were dropped when my mother decided to move us back to Minnesota. I swear the only thing they wanted was us out of their hair! I continued to get into trouble in Minnesota by doing basically the same things I was doing in California. The county assigned a social worker to work with me because they thought I was self-destructive.

"I have a lot of family problems and get into trouble because of them. My mother tries to dominate me and I have to rebel. I won't be a puppet. I'm going to make my own decisions about life. If you can never please someone why would you knock yourself out trying? My mom is going crazy over what I just did but she goes crazy over anything I do. I have been performing negative behaviors and now I'm in here. That's it!"

COMMENTARY

The beginning of her essay reveals a potential for creativity of expression. Hopefully, this can be developed in a self-enhancing way. An alcoholic mother with whom there is an apparent lack of communication is an unhealthy foundation for any child. Her mother may have unrealistic expectations, feeding Audrey's perception that she can never live up to her mother's standards. Why try to please a mother with whom there is much unidentified hostility? Their conflict is obviously very deep and it might not be healthy for them to be together. Unfortunately, Audrey has no contact with other relatives; alone, she is incapable of making positive decisions about her life.

To exchange home for a life leading to prostitution would make absolutely no sense to the average person. Imagine how extremely painful home must be if girls are willing to leave that for a precarious life on the road. Prostitution is fraught with dangers on all sides. The police constantly seek to protect these young girls and are patently regarded as the enemy--the one positive hope these girls have. Today, the murder of a young girl in a motel no longer makes front-page news. Bodies are constantly being found in the desert and dismissed with the description, "believed to be female prostitute."

The ultimate provocateur in the life of a prostitute is the person for whom she toils, the pimp. He will tolerate her existence as long as she stays healthy and productive. Even then, she is subject to beatings and other forms of intimidation. She exists only to please her pimp and to make money for him. As long as she is capable of that she will be clothed, fed, and taken from city to city to perform her tasks.

The Magdalene Project in Van Nuys, CA., and the Genesis House in Chicago, Ill., mentioned earlier in this chapter, confirm that most of the women with whom they work have experienced severe childhood abuse, often sexual. Abuse has many forms and the emotional abuse that many of these youngsters endure is as debilitating as any. For these girls it is clear, they would rather be involved in prostitution than in incest or other abuse at home. Though the rewards are slight and the risks formidable there is a perverse sense of security--a sense of belonging, albeit tentative.

Adele Weiner, Associate Dean of the Wurzweiler School of Social Work, Yeshiva University, cited their study of nearly 2,000 New York streetwalkers (L.A.Times, 12/2/96): A shocking 35 percent tested positive for HIV--and on average had two children. Given the ambivalence toward helping these young women, their grave medical picture does not bode well for their children or ultimately society at large. As long as prostitution is treated strictly as a criminal problem and the social aspects are ignored the girls involved remain trapped in a hopeless situation. We must open the door to <u>all</u> the social programs available if we are going to rescue these desperate people!

Chapter 6

ABUSE NEGLECT
Desperate Cries For Help

Literally, who must bear the responsibly for protecting children who suffer abuse or neglect or both? When tragedy occurs, members of society (law enforcement, social workers, parents, etc.) often point fingers at one another. Rarely does any one person or group take responsibility. When situations reach crisis point the juvenile court judge must intervene and bestow his final jurisdiction. But before this legal intervention, many agencies are involved as child abuse is happening.

Social workers, teachers, care providers, recreation directors and coaches, medical personnel, and police are <u>all</u> required to report signs of abuse or neglect. In most states, a state agency is the ultimate overseer of the county agencies. The question is, with so many people involved in the protection of children how can so much be missed or ignored?

As a former teacher and school principal, I know how difficult it is to discuss these incogitable problems with the children themselves. What if you further frighten them or destroy their confidence? <u>Reporting</u> signs of abuse in a household could embitter the child toward the adult he thinks reported the incident. As challenging as this is, it must be faced. We have to make the process of reporting problems one that children, as well as adults, can do without fear or apprehension. As professional caretakers, we must imbue trust and confidence. These two qualities are the keys to working effectively with abused children.

Once an initial investigation is done by the protective agency, there must be a full-scale, cooperative effort among all governmental agencies. Judges, social workers, and medical personnel must all work as a team to adequately safeguard and protect each and every child who may be or acutely is in danger.

In Michigan an "actuarial" system determines the degree of

safety the home must provide. Danger to children is based on a point system which measures a variety of factors: domestic violence, substance abuse, living conditions, school participation, physical and medical conditions.

However, objective ratings are rare. Agencies often deflect criticism of their operation by shifting blame or responsibility elsewhere. This is cynically referred to as CYA (cover yourself, deflect guilt). This occurs when agency personnel fail to properly assess the hazards a child in their care is confronting. Sandra Thompson of The Las Vegas Sun writes about a principal and teacher who "received a letter from a deputy attorney general telling them they did not follow Nevada Revised Statutes 432B. He said they failed to immediately report child abuse. They had reported it several times." (Editorial Page, 1/3/98) It must be pointed out that the professionals who deal with abuse and neglect are among the most understaffed and overworked people in the system. Having said this, the following stories are filled with situations which someone in the bureaucracy should have corrected but did not.

DEWANNA'S STORY

I can't imagine anyone who looks more out of place in detention than Dewanna. Her naturally stunning appearance makes even drab institutional clothing look fashionable. Abrupt with everyone, she is called "snippy" by her peers. To earn her trust you need a very gentle and consistent approach.

Meticulous in everything that she did, her beautiful handwriting was a joy to read. Dewanna would become extremely agitated if anyone, particularly one of the boys, even nominally disrupted her studies. She'd return a smile with a frown. Aware she harbored much hostility, she had not come to grips with its innermost origins. CHARGES: curfew, obstruction public police officer, possession stolen vehicle, conspiracy to commit burglary, U.I./controlled substance

DEWANNA: ESSAY #28

"I was born in the hospital emergency room. My mother was nineteen years old, unmarried, and not sure where we would put our heads to rest when we got out. I am the result of a one night encounter. My mother is black and my father is Italian. I have never spoken to nor seen my father, even in a picture, so I have no idea what he looks like.

"After I was born I lived with my mother who tried to raise me on her own as a single parent. I was removed from her home by the state at age five. I was taken away after it was discovered that my mother's boyfriend, who is now the father of my ten year old brother, had been sexually abusing me since age three.

"I was placed in an institution called Child Haven and subsequently transferred to several different group homes where I lived for most of my life.

"I was always considered a bright child and was placed in a class for gifted children at age seven. I did very well academically in school but always had problems as far as my behavior. I was disruptive in class, disrespectful of others, and generally abusive to my peers. I was often asked why I was such an angry child. That is a question I never answered for anyone. I didn't even know myself!

"At age twelve I started getting in trouble with the law. After a number of mostly status offenses my probation was revoked and I was sent to the youth center for correctional programming. I stayed for five months and came out worse than when I went in. I learned a lot of things in the Center; some good, some bad.

"I did O.K. for a while after I was released but only because I had become sneakier and wasn't caught doing anything for a while. They caught on to that act and sent me back after being out for ten and one half months. They also sent me back a third time after only a two month release. The third time was just about a year ago.

"Throughout my year on the outs this is the first time I've been in trouble. This will be my last time here because I will turn eighteen in three months.

"Hopefully, I will get my GED before I get out so that I can get a job when I'm released. There must be a job out there that pays well. I've worked before and know already I would have no problem handling something at an entry level in the medical field.

"Once I save enough for college tuition I plan to enroll at community college and after two years go to the university. Hopefully, I can find a good counselor who will help me with finances. I plan to graduate from college and become a professional in the field of medicine."

COMMENTARY:

Dewanna will obviously need a great deal of help, but it's also equally obvious she has the intelligence and drive to accomplish her goals. Her file is heavy with status offenses sprinkled with a few more serious violations. Drugs played a role in her life, but not the major role it does in most incarcerated children. However, if her circumstances dictate an urgency for money, she is likely to do whatever is necessary. With the guidance available to her and her current positive attitude, this should be fairly easy for her to avoid.

Child abuse must be dealt with vigorously and immediately! We have no choice. The long-term effects on abused children are vividly devastating. Most of the 969,000 confirmed cases of child abuse for 1996 were reported by teachers, police, doctors, family members, or neighbors. The privately funded National Committee to Prevent Child Abuse issued an in-depth report based on these 1996 figures, which revealed the following: 60 percent of profound neglect involved children left unsupervised, usually by parents with alcohol or drug problems, 23 percent involved physical abuse, and nine percent sexual abuse. These children depend heavily on the professionals within the community as the main deterrence of this debasement.

A fourteen year-old Miami girl wrote a simple five line poem that indicated she was being abused. Her English teacher, alarmed, looked in her class assigned journal and saw this entry: "Lord I'm tired of being RAPED!!! I can't do nothing about it cause I'm too damn AFRAID!!! HELP ME PLEASE!!!". This was reported in The Review Journal/Sun (11-4-97). The article said the teacher contacted state abuse authorities and the girl's uncle was arrested and jailed.

Dewanna languished in a sexually abusive situation for nearly two years. She was finally removed from the household after a neighbor persistently kept reporting her suspicions for over a year! Her mother and her live-in boyfriend were both criminally negligent, yet neither of them were ever tried for these offenses! Dewanna will forever bear the scars of her abuse. I'm certain she knows why she was such an angry child and why, as she approaches adulthood, this anger still spews forth. The 1996 report on child abuse and neglect stated that sexual abuse represented a chilling 87,000 children during that one-year period alone.

NALISA'S STORY

The oldest of ten children, NaLisa has always felt the need to be the role model for her siblings, which she does fairly well. Despite her troubled circumstances, she didn't careen off course until she rebelled in a rage over her grandmother's stern, unbending religious convictions. She tried to bridge the generation gap, be everything her grandmother demanded as well as attend school and take advantage of extra-curricular activities. Sadly, NaLisa couldn't juggle all these responsibilities. CHARGES: provoking assault, violating probation, curfew, false information

NALISA: ESSAY #29

"I was born up north in Washington and lived there about two years. My mother and father moved from place to place and with only one child, me, it was pretty easy to relocate and find new jobs. Then we suddenly grew to be a big family with six girls and four boys. My mother always wanted ten children. I'm the first of the ten, the oldest.

"I knew I had to be a good role model for all my sisters and brothers. It was hard because my parents weren't being good role models for me. My father started drinking alcohol and then my mother. Then my father started using heavy drugs like cocaine, heroin, pot and others.

"Drugs triggered something in my dad's head and he started abusing my mother for her money so he could get high with his friends. Soon we didn't have no food to eat or no place to lay our heads so we had to panhandle for money. Sometimes we slept in parks and sometimes in homeless shelters.

"My mother wasn't as bad on drugs and alcohol as my father was. She used to look at us kids and try to hide the money so we could have something to eat or a place to lay our heads. My father suspected what she was doing and made my mother take all her clothes off so he could look for money. Sometimes he would even do us the same way.

"My mother and father was together for eleven years. Finally my mother got tired of my father taking everything for drugs and made a plan. Very quietly one night she called my grandmother and asked if she could possibly come and get us. My grandmother lived in another state but she said to just wait quietly and sure nuff two days later she came for us.

"I was so happy to get out of that nightmare we were living in! I told my brothers and sisters how we were going to stay with our grandmother and they were overjoyed and ready to go. Grandmother put us in school and took us shopping for clothes.

"I was very happy and so was my whole family. The only hitch was my mother. She was still doing drugs and to give money to my grandmother she started prostituting. My grandmother said she had already set it up so she was getting a check for us and didn't want my mom's money, period!

"My grandmother is a devout Christian and has been all her life. This made it hard because when I started going to junior and senior high school people started making fun of me because I had to wear skirts every day to school. It was against her religion for a lady to wear pants. She's been like that her whole life.

"Every morning when I got ready for school I used to sneak shorts on up under my skirt. Before I got on the bus I would take my skirt off and go to school.

"One day my grandmother saw me. She called me in the house and hit me with her belt like two hundred times. She told me that she was going to take me out of track and basketball. It was always hard to get her to sign for me. I begged her to leave me in.

"Nothing worked so I started running away to my friend's house because I thought my grandmother wasn't being fair. This set off a series of trips from foster home to foster home because if I couldn't participate at school I was running away.

"I eventually told my social worker that I wanted to move back with my mother. The social worker found my mother and started giving her drug tests. She had to be off drugs and alcohol if I was allowed to stay with her again. All of my mother's tests were clean because she said she wanted me back. I got to stay with my mother again!

"It had been many years since I had seen my dad so I decided to go looking for him. I found him and he was doing great. He had got off drugs and started a new life as a minister of a church. I hope things work out so I can stay reunited with both of my parents. My sisters and brothers are still living with our grandmother but I just know one of these days I'll see them again."

COMMENTARY

NaLisa's caseworkers felt there'd be a positive ending to this story. Both parents, though leading entirely separate lives, had miraculously rid themselves of their addiction to drugs and alcohol and became productive, employed individuals.

NeLisa felt very anxious to reconnect with her siblings, which had not happened when I saw her last. She had the talent to play sports and run track at the collegiate level. In excellent physical condition, she had no record of abusing drugs or alcohol. Her academic skills are slightly below average but her determination should easily compensate for that obstacle. She hasn't appeared on the local sports page yet but with girl's sports getting increased newspaper coverage, I will be watching track and basketball closely.

Unfortunately, most of the stories in this chapter will not have a positive ending. NaLisa and her family are the exception to the rule. Too many stories deal with life from an entirely different perspective.

DEEDEE'S STORY

DeeDee's mother used drugs during her pregnancy--an inauspicious beginning for any child. Although she did not exhibit most of the descriptors of a 'snow baby', DeeDee did exhibit behavior at times which defied description. Erratic, she would work fairly well with high-interest-level material if she had no distractions.

She couldn't escape abusive relationships and they've had an adverse impact on many aspects of her life. She has a baby in her troubled life, which she is totally incapable of nurturing emotionally or physically.

An average-sized Caucasian female, she has an intellectual disposition, always reading and asking questions about everything that piques her interest. You sense many unspoken questions which are part of her desperate attempt to unravel her own identity. CHARGES: solicitation for prostitution, obstructing public officer, minor in bar, curfew

DEEDEE: ESSAY #30

"When I was born my mom was doing drugs and really wanted to get rid of me. My dad would not let her. They kept on fighting with each other over having children but still managed to have my sister a year and one-half later.

"My mom said she wanted to have an abortion with my sister but my dad said he would not stand for that. He said he wanted to take care of me and my sister if she didn't.

"They separated but my mom wouldn't let him take us with him. I don't know why because she never took care of us. When

I was two years old my mom left me and my sister in the house for five days alone. My sister really got sick. My dad came by the house. He could hear us crying so he broke down the door and grabbed me and my sister.

"I guess the nextdoor neighbor heard all the noise and called the police. My dad explained everything and the police let my father go. When my mom came by for us my dad beat her up so bad she had to go into the hospital.

"They managed to get back together after that but split up again when I turned three years old. My dad left the state and left me and my sister with my mother. He wasn't gone long before she found a boyfriend . He was always hitting me because he didn't like to hear me crying. Both he and my mom were on drugs and gave very little attention to me and my sister. When I turned four my mom left me and my sister with a babysitter and never came back!

"My grandmother came and picked us up and called the police. They called my dad and asked him to come to court for me and my sister if he wanted to get custody. He got custody and took us both back to Tucson with him.

"When we got there we lived with him and his girlfriend. She had five children so we were all crowded into this little place. We lived there for several years. Finally his girlfriend got tired of him beating her and had the police kick us out.

"We decided to come back here and that is when my dad really began to drink a lot. He would hit me and my sister when he was drinking. It got so bad we were placed in foster care. I kept running away but they would catch me and lock me up pending placement in a different foster home. They continuously switched me from home to home. That's when I lost all hope and started doing drugs.

"I got beat over drugs and locked up. They could beat me all they wanted but I still did drugs. This went on for three years and the foster home people finally said they were through.

"I was nearly sixteen the last time they locked me up. I was five and one half months pregnant and stayed in confinement until I was seven and one half months pregnant. I was getting so big they couldn't keep me locked down so I went to a group home and had my baby. From there they put me in Independent Living. I didn't like the restrictions and ran. I was on my own for over five months when they caught me and put me in here. My baby is in foster care and I don't know what I'm going to do!"

COMMENTARY

Nearly eighteen, DeeDee cannot care for herself properly; adding a baby begs disaster. Deserted by the baby's father, she is alone and on her own. The courts must decide if she is capable of being reunited with her baby, who will remain in foster care. Social workers grapple with trying to balance the rights of parents versus their obligation to protect children. The ramifications of drug abuse further complicate this equation, which now tends to be the cardinal factor governing their decision-making. The California Judiciary Committee reported that child welfare workers estimate from 70 to 90 percent of all abuse and neglect cases stem from a drug addicted parent or family unit (1995 statistic).

Throughout America today a wide variety of laws are being reviewed which deal with abuse and neglect of children. For example, should a judge have the option to cease all efforts to keep the family intact after the second proven case of abuse? On the surface, this seems entirely reasonable. However, like the 'three strike law' this needs to be approached with caution. Would it survive the challenge to a higher court?

One of the most critical factors in curbing abuse is removing an abusive, violent parent (or other adult) from the household. Incredibly, this is difficult to do in many states. Clearly, this is crucial to the safety of the children. In a special to the Washington Post, Patrick Fagan writes: "We need to get kids out of abusive homes as soon as possible--permanently, if the situation merits it. Children can recover from the trauma of abuse and thrive, but not until they are provided a stable--and loving-- environment. Efforts to reunite abused children with their families-- the bedrock principle behind child protective services in most states--should be continued, but we need to be more willing to abandon efforts when they are not working" (Las Vegas Sun, 9-14-97).

How strange that a household which appears to be the stereotypical home embodying the American dream, overnight resembles a scene from a horror movie. Like a firecracker, some households seem to explode of their own volition, wreaking havoc as they do so.

WREN'S STORY

Once Wren seemed to be a part of the American dream home with a stable family life and all the positive fringe benefits implied. Today he has the stern look of a hardened criminal, the antithesis of that setting. At six-foot, this muscled Caucasian youth has the scarred look of a survivor of the streets. His life changed drastically when his father ran off, taking the family stability with him. CHARGES: bench warrant served, curfew, battery police officer, possession controlled substance, distribution controlled substance, possession firearms

WREN: ESSAY #31

"My name is Wren. I was born in Wisconsin and my parents named me after my grandfather, mayor of the city. They brought me home to this nice little house and eventually, two brothers too. My pre-teenage years are the fondest years of my life. My mother and father both had jobs and we were a happy middle-class family.

"By the time I was thirteen my mother was in the Wisconsin State Penitentiary for armed robbery. She had lost her job and my father ran off. She felt responsible for everything and robbed a Seven/Eleven to feed and house us kids. When the police caught up with her, me and my two brothers split and struck out on our own!

"We had no legal way to survive so we started selling drugs, crack cocaine to be exact. We made some money and got a place to crash. Meanwhile, my brother Wendell got busted a few times and was looking at serious jail time. He got real nervous so we bought bus tickets and headed out to California.

"When we got there things were not as easy as we thought. It wasn't as easy selling dope in California as in Wisconsin. There were cops all over and a lot more competition. I was only fifteen but I knew it was getting hot there and we had better move on. One week before we planned the move, Wendell sold to an undercover and got locked up. He was sentenced to a year in the C.Y.A. (California Youth Authority). I supported me and my little brother for almost a year and then I got busted.

"My little brother was sent back to Wisconsin to live with relatives while I was locked up in California serving eight months. The authorities discovered my dad was living here and sent me to live with him.

"My older brother, who had been released from C.Y.A., was out on the streets and being real crazy. They said he just didn't care any more and died of a heroin overdose. I couldn't take the loss so I kind of went crazy and ended up here. Getting arrested probably saved my life!"

COMMENTARY

Wren has few skills other than those he learned on the streets. He needs to be incarcerated until he stabilizes himself and learns academic or vocational skills. A very likable and extremely personable young man, he is articulate in stating his need for help. He will benefit from his nine to twelve month sentence in the state institution. However, that may not be enough time for him to stabilize. He is a ship without a rudder at this stage of his life.

BILLY'S STORY

Many youths in detention never had close contact with their parents from birth. In fact, Billy was born in a prison hospital. (His father and mother were serving time for either murder or attempted murder.) Billy, who never knew his parents, is aware of where he was born and the dire circumstances in which he entered the world.

States are now passing laws that will allow judges to cut parental rights in specific cases, especially where a violent felony conviction, extensive drug abuse, or heavy addiction to alcohol is involved. Billy's parents fit this description. His mother also suffered from extensive mental problems.

Billy's body language warns you not to come too close. You sense immediately he does not trust you and will question everything you say. He looked like a young man who had physically defended himself many times and would readily do so again. His crude tattoos pointed to gang involvement, but his blond hair and baby face refuted that connection. However, his cold stare reinstated the gang connection. CHARGES: burglary/two counts, robbery/use deadly weapon, concealed weapon, possession stolen property

BILLY: ESSAY #32

"I guess my story would have to begin when I was born in a prison hospital somewhere in the eastern part of the country. I can't remember my mother or father that much. Hell, around the age of about two I was given to the state by my mom who hoped that I would get a place to stay while she worked out her marriage problems. My mother had been diagnosed with the symptoms of schizophrenia and other mental problems.

"I was placed with the court and sent to Child Haven where I grew up until I was about four. I had never lived in a house and that is what they were trying to find for me. It was finally found and they placed me in a foster home. Basically a foster home is a home where a kid has a new family and can stay for as long as that family wants them. According to state welfare you can adopt a foster kid after a certain amount of time.

"They really want to get a feel of how the kid acts. You can have a short term or long term foster home and they even have a pediatric home for infants and young children. These are all based on how--and if--the people want to have a new family.

"Well, I saw them all and hated all houses, all homes, and all families! I will admit to being a little rascal when they moved me around. Basically, it is not the fact that I suffered psychological problems but something deeper.

"Think about this! How would you feel after your parents gave you up to strangers for the rest of your life? It's not a day in the park. I can tell you that much!

"They want to break through your Achilles heel. They want you to give up. They want you to surrender to welfare or to the state. You sometimes want to, but they set off a trigger in your mind. That trigger says you can't leave and can't ever get out. That makes you want to fight it all the more. Most kids end up in prison. I think I know why. These places mess with your mind too much!"

COMMENTARY

From an early age Billy seemed on a fast track for prison and no one could do much to slow the progression. With absolutely no ties to anyone in the world, he felt extremely bitter about his fate. He felt cheated, deserted by everyone with whom he had contact while growing up. We talked several times, and I have never encountered a boy who needed intervention so desperately.

Some states have created an office which acts as a children's guardian agency. These are independent and non-partisan, but still within the purview of the state agency that protects children. Having the authority to intervene on behalf of children in dependency cases, they are especially important to damaged youngsters like Billy. I served as a surrogate parent to several children assigned to juvenile court and found this rewarding and extremely important to the juveniles involved.

The protection agencies are constantly being urged to act more swiftly in cases of physical and sexual abuse. Girls in particular are often returned to the setting where the abuse occurred. Lawanda Ravoira, director of PACE, a nonresidential therapeutic counseling program, confirms this: "What I constantly hear from well-intentioned juvenile judges is 'We have nowhere to send her'"(L.A.Times, 7-9-96). Thus returning her to the same environment. Because most of the delinquents in the system are boys, the little funding available is usually spent on facilities for boys.

We are profoundly <u>underreacting</u> to the abuse of children throughout the system. Initially, we must streamline how such problems are recorded, share medical histories with all involved agencies and then take immediate action when any abuse is suspected. An average of five to six children are killed each day by an abusive parent or the parent's live-in boyfriend. (1993 Statistic, National Incidence Study, U.S. Department of Health and Human Services)

PAM'S STORY

Pam is a poignant example of a child who has endured sexual abuse most of her life with no record of any agency or individual intervention. Her mother must have known something about this abuse since it continued for thirteen years.

An attractive black girl, Pam's radiant smile transcended the human despair she had suffered throughout her childhood. Literally imprisoned in an unresponsive household, she lives utterly devoid of self-pity which is a testament to the beauty of the human spirit. Her sprightly humor reveals a resiliency that will sustain her throughout her life, obviously this quality has helped her survive without totally crushing her spirit.

Most children share their dark secrets with at least one person in their life. It seems impossible this perverted behavior went on undeterred for over a dozen years! CHARGES: solicitation for prostitution, robbery, grand larceny attempt, false information

PAM: ESSAY #33

"I was born seventeen years ago to a mother not really prepared to take care of me. I never was around my father but spent the first thirteen years of my life with Mom and her boyfriend. I will refer to them as my parents.

"At the age of one I was being molested by my mother's highschool boyfriend. As long as I can remember this continued to go on until I was thirteen. It is strange but in spite of him molesting me in nearly every way, I was still a virgin when I turned fourteen.

"I was raped when I was fourteen but never told my parents and to this day they still don't know. It caused me to have nightmares but I just kept them to myself except for my best friend.

"When I was fifteen I ran away from home for the second time. The first time I was living with my grandmother and great-grandmother. The second time that I ran away I left with my friend and we went over to the Boulevard. That's where I met James. James and I met several more times before we actually got together. You know, together! It was a sure connection!

"I started getting into trouble about two weeks before I met James. I know it sounds like James is the main reason that I get in so much trouble. He is not. My problems with stealing and prostitution are my fault and no one else's. James did not put me on the tracks! Be serious. I stole things strictly for me!"

COMMENTARY

After suffering sexual abuse for so many years with no one to rescue her, it is ironic that the first time she escaped and hit the "tracks" she was taken into protective custody. This is a disturbing revelation about our priorities. An example, again, of how professional advocacy is not doing what must be done to protect children.

Soliciting sex for money is called being on the tracks. While the girls had a variety of explanations for the term, none seemed to know exactly what it meant. Yet, this phrase was used by most of the girls who engaged in prostitution, thinly disguising what they actually did. An insidious, dangerous form of defilement prostitution is a Machiavellian morass that shrouds these girls in a horrible cloak of danger. How can they treat it in such a cavalier manner?

Dealing with all the formidable issues of abuse and neglect is an extremely complex and demanding responsibility. In many states judges may lack formal training in juvenile problems, and deal mainly with adult crime. On a given day a judge may handle a divorce, a business litigation, and a complex juvenile case. Seldom does one judge have expertise in all areas. Yet crucial decisions concerning a juvenile's future often are made by judges with good intent but little knowledge.

There is a strong and apparent need to develop child abuse education and training standards for Juvenile Court judges.

Too many cases are being mishandled in courts throughout the nation. Perhaps we should prohibit judges from hearing child-dependency cases until they have taken classes which will help them demonstrate knowledge and understanding of these unique problems.

CHILD NEGLECT

Neglect is an easily ignored form of abuse unless the child is living under such deprived conditions that they scream for attention. Superficial neglect often takes the form of parental disregard. Parents ignore the problems as they magnify and grow. Are such parents willingly abdicating their responsibilities to the court? These avoidance symptoms show up in parents who profess to be helpless, vulnerable victims of a juvenile out of control. This aversion to responsibility is all too prevalent among parents of damaged youngsters.

FRED'S STORY

Children complain about parents who expect perfection and how oppressive that can be. Equally oppressive is neglect that spawns an awareness that neither one of their parents really cares about them. Fred, who becomes alternately angry then depressed about his self-destructive behavior, regards his parents as major contributors to his situation. He feels they have consistently abdicated their responsibilities.

At first glance, he seems to fit the gang mold perfectly, although he's a rather frail Caucasian youth who's unimposing physically. The crude, ink-scratched tattoos on the knuckles of both hands speak of his gang affiliation as do the tattoos on his forearms, which carry the markings of his gang.

His first day in school he is strangely animated. It is soon obvious he is trying to covertly throw gang signs (hand signals) to students who pass by the interior windows of the classroom. This was not tolerated within the school/court rules and I had to have a discussion with him. His explanation? He was just glad to see his "brother." A counselor confirmed this was the extent of his signals--essentially an acknowledgment in gang-hand-style language. He'd willingly risk a twenty-four hour lock-down, standard punishment for throwing gang signs, simply to acknowledge a fellow gang member. His gang affiliation was unmistakably the pre-eminent force in his life. CHARGES: burglary, possession controlled substance, gang enhancement

FRED: ESSAY #34

I was born in Illinois and spent the first four years of my life living happily with my mom and dad. After I turned four, I guess my mom didn't feel like sticking around. She moved out and left me for my dad to look after.

"Two years later I started school and had a really hard time. My friend didn't like it either so we decided it was just easier to skip school. My dad finally caught us and was he mad! I didn't know what to expect, but didn't think he would ship me out to my mom. I've been living with her ever since...end of story for Dad. I have never seen him since. My mother has finally accepted me into her life but doesn't spend a lot of time with me. I do pretty much what I want to do.

"I've been in a bit of trouble with the police since I moved here. My friends and I used to skip school and go to the mall. We got caught stealing and were confined in the temporary lockup area of detention. My mom had to come and pick me up. All she said is that I'm nine years old and I need to change.

"Around my eleventh birthday I got arrested again, this time for having a B.B. gun and a bike that was stolen. My mom didn't even care. Since she didn't care, I started hanging around Gip who was like an older brother to me. I ran with him and started getting into fights and earning my reputation for being a punk!

"I actually got tired of that and started settling down some. I tried to stop doing most of the things getting me into trouble. That, however, did not last long. When I was fifteen I got jumped into this gang. We all did drugs, robbed houses, and other rotten things.

"Now I'm seventeen. The same stuff I was doing at fifteen and just getting a slap on the wrist has landed me in here. When I get out I don't plan on doing any of it any more. I have a son now and I don't want him turning out like me. I want to be there for him so he don't make the same mistakes that I did."

COMMENTARY

Fred does not give his girlfriend or his child any monetary support. His relationship with the child centers around visits of an hour or less on a staggered random basis. The fact he is not welcomed by the mother's parents complicates the situation. Her parents have urged her to place the child for adoption, which she has steadfastly refused to do. The baby has physical problems, no doubt caused by drug use by both parents. Fred understands the child places a strain on her family. He believes that she will either place the child for adoption or be asked to leave. He assumes she will opt to leave her family and he wants to be there when she does.

Agencies which must deal with these situations are challenged to alleviate the entangled assortment of difficulties that inevitably arise from such unhealthy alliances among youths. When a child is added to an already troubled environment, these cases become extremely complicated and impact a variety of agencies. They often work side by side but not together. The schools as well as welfare and other agencies must expand access to each other so that all professionals work together with adequate information and coordinate their efforts to end the cycle of youthful parental irresponsibility.

Violence is a thoroughly ingrained component of delinquent boys and girls. Even during incarceration, most have no other resource when a conflict arises. Cottage counselors in juvenile detention spend much of their time in conflict avoidance: locking down combatants, imposing time-outs when conflicts intensify, restricting movement when warranted, and much more. So much of their time is spent in maintenance, they rarely have time to work with youngsters in more positive ways: teaching management of anger or effective interpersonal skills.

CHIP'S STORY

Chip, who just turned seventeen, has a deep-seated problem with his violent nature. Inflicting pain has been a way of life for him his entire existence. Anger and self-control counseling have been fairly successful in helping him resolve minor conflicts without getting physical. But he absolutely needs continued and intensive therapy.

Chip is not a big, imposing physical specimen and because of this he is often underestimated. Mostly a loner, only two black detainees comprise his very small circle of friends. They described him as having "devil eyes"--when angry, eyes narrowed and unblinking, the description fits. His whole aura screams: "BACK OFF!" CHARGES: burglary, attempted grand larceny, obstruction police officer, resisting arrest, battery, assault

CHIP: ESSAY #35

"When I was born my father said I had a well-developed future ahead of me. I don't know what he meant by that but so far my life has not been "well developed." The first half of my life I spent in Oregon where my mother worked. In elementary school I was considered a bright student.

"My father had gone to the Carolinas and surrounding states to live but he still kept in contact with us. Complications occurred in Oregon so I left to live with my father. We lived in that area off and on for about six years, mostly because that is where his beloved mother lived.

"Somewhere during all of this I took a violent turn down the wrong road. Hurting people, battery, and revenge just came naturally to me. I would laugh and brag about the terror I saw in my enemies eyes.

"I was in New Orleans for Mardi Gras and decided things were a little too hot so I took a flight out and came here to be with my mother. I was having too many problems back there and hoped my mom might be able to help.

"I arrived during my freshman year in high school. My first year there were no problems because I was committed to the Anger and Self-Control Group, a counseling association. I slacked off the next year because my mother moved into an area that had a lot of gang activity. They would pressure me to resolve my problems violently.

"I have never lived the life of crime but the crowd I associate with has. Peer pressure has always been an everyday thing. But I started growing and maturing and learning responsibility for my actions. I have to let peers assume their own lives and just live my own. That is the only way you reach your goals in life.

"When you travel the road you sometimes stumble too far and have to pay. I'm in here for two counts of battery with substantial bodily harm and two counts of robbery. When you stumble and fall you can't let yourself fail! I'll brush myself off and go on with my life and my goals."

COMMENTARY

Whether or not he can "brush himself off" and continue in a non-violent manner is a smoldering issue. Despite optimistic forecasts from his counselor, he is sometimes consumed with self-doubt. He exhibits control for brief periods, then collides violently with animosity. Counseling, incarceration, and school are his existence for the next eight to twelve months. If his expected growth in anger control and educational attainment materialize the prognosis for his future could be very positive.

Our communities have become especially dangerous for law enforcement as well as for individual citizens. This is an alarming and ominous occurrence. Children who come from families where abuse and neglect are rampant are most apt to become part of the criminal underbelly of society and contributors to it.

Abuse and neglect of children are major issues which affect profoundly many households throughout the nation. New laws that emphasize innovative approaches to this problem are desperately needed. The police are increasingly confronting more violent and well-armed criminals. In Las Vegas, for example, the number of police officers killed in the line of duty during the previous year increased a chilling 27 percent! (Las Vegas Sun, 1-4-98)

We must break the cycle of abuse and neglect so that the next generation of children do not follow in the footsteps of their parents. This extremely complex and challenging task must be treated with urgency. President Clinton's 1997 Federal report on America's youth, compiled by a consortium of federal agencies, showed several important gains offset by negative trends in drug and tobacco use, an upsurge in violent crime, and a dramatic increase, 5 percent in 1950 to 32 percent in 1995, in unmarried mothers. The key gains were in such important areas as nutrition, mortality, and educational attainment.

Children must hear clear messages on the dangers of using drugs, including alcohol and tobacco use. If these messages do not come from their parents we must make certain the community is there to bring the message to them. We must utilize innovative programs, such as the TOP program, described in the next paragraph, and identify others that are being successfully utilized across the nation.

Nurturing is an ongoing and crucial part of a child's being. Volunteers are recruited to cuddle children in the intensive care units of hospitals when parents are not available. The human touch is still essential for the baby's survival. The Teen Outreach Program (TOP), started nearly two decades ago and spread to 120 classrooms in 25 cities, is also involved in nurturing babies. The teens cuddle colicky crack babies and change their dirty diapers. In a recent study these teen girls had an astounding 40 percent fewer pregnancies than those measured in a control group (U.S. News & World Report, 12-29-97). University psychologist Joseph Allen reports that "What this program does is change kids' perception about themselves and tells them they have a role in the community."

Lastly, teachers, social workers, judges and others must work harder and more effectively at spotting problems such as severe depression, dejection, dispiritedness and lact of vitality that lead young people to make destructive lifestyle decisions. We must use our limited resources wisely if we are to make a dent in the burgeoning juvenile-related problems confronting this nation.

Chapter 7

"GANGSTER" PROSE & POETRY
Creative Endeavors

In my work with incarcerated youths, I discovered, to my surprise that boys are more likely than girls to reveal their deepest thoughts. Boys write about the need for understanding, intimacy, guidance, or simply a pledge that someone close will wait for them. Being locked up in a cell is a helpless feeling. It is hard to look down a dark tunnel and keep that tiny light in perspective. These kids often lose contact with those who are most meaningful to their lives. They rely on parents or close relatives to transmit their intimate messages.

Unlike their peers on the outside, you won't hear them animatedly discussing their careers or how they'll generate income in certain fields of interest. The best way to explore and understand the disintegration of societal values and behavior is to listen to these locked-up youngsters speak in animated tones about drugs, crime, even graffiti.

When they started the writing exercise for GED prep I urged them to write about what most concerned them, and about things in which they felt they had expertise. Some of these essays and poems are included in this chapter.

The first poem, "A Gangster's Prayer," in a dozen similar versions, has been circulating through the cottages. The poetry focuses on the issues these teens love and fear; and on the guidance they need to make a leviathan change in their lives.

A GANGSTER'S PRAYER

Heavenly Father, please hear me tonight,
I need so much guidance to live my life right.
Sometimes the pressure is too much to bear,
I often wonder, does anyone care?
How can I wake up and face a new day.
Knowing I have to live my life this crazy way.

Heavenly Father, forgive all my sins.
I want to change but where do I begin?
Give me the strength to resist the wild life
I desire.
Help me get away from the nightly gunfire.
Please God, bless my family whose eyes silently plead
For me not to go out, as they watch me leave.

God, bless my mother who cries every night,
Worrying I'll be killed in yet another gang fight.
Heavenly Father, please answer my prayer.
Please let me know that you are still listening up there.
When will it end? What is it for?
To prove to my homies, yeah, I'm hard core?
Sometimes I even wonder how will I die,
A bullet wound or a knife will I buy?

Heavenly Father, please hear me tonight.
Give me the courage and strength to live my life right!
Please show me the way, Lord, show me the light.
Help give my heart peace so I don't have to fight.
Thank you for your forgiveness Lord!
Thank you for being there for one of the hoard!
Thank you for listening to this sinner's prayer,

The next poem "Young and Lost" surfaced when I returned to teaching in 1991, and it is still making the rounds. This poem captures their lack of dreams and aspirations.

YOUNG AND LOST

I am young and lost in this crazy world.
I wonder if tomorrow will be worth living?
I hear no evil.
I see no evil.
I want to feel love that I don't have.
I am young and lost in this crazy world.
I pretend not to care for anything.

I feel despair losing the only love I had;
the only love I cared and felt for!
I touch the gates of heaven and then fall
back down in this burning hell!
I worry about living and about my death.
I cry because this world is so chaotic.
I am young and proud and lost in this crazy world.
I understand things can't always go my way.
I will say things I shouldn't say.
I try to find a way out of this abyss
I hope I can achieve my goals in this dark world.
I am young and lost in this dark and crazy world!

COMMENTARY

A fundamental lamentation describes how much they miss their family and other loved ones. The liaison for which they pine grows in meaning and depth with each week they spend in detention. Their romantic relationships often dry up like last week's flowers as the separation takes its toll. "I Miss You" is written by a boy who has been in detention long enough to have a lot of regrets while savoring some tender memories.

I MISS YOU

I miss you like the nights without stars
I miss you like the roses miss spring.
Without you, I feel everything is coming to an end!
Your love dwells in my mind and hides in my heart.
Now that you're gone I feel the world is different.
The sunshine has disappeared and the rains have started.
Falling like the tears on my pillow each night.
I think of you. I miss you.
I miss the day your smile awakened my heart.
I miss you!

COMMENTARY

The next piece is a lament aimed at someone who means a great deal to this person. The wait increases his anxiety and insecurity: "Will her feelings remain strong?" he wonders. Nothing is lonelier than a cold desolate cell. Stark and impersonal, it is not a pleasant place to contemplate one's life.

PLEASE WAIT

Wedding cake
Under the stars
Mistake, sit behind bars
Love we make Believe
Believe, take Leave
Life at stake

Heart
Months Apart
Once Kiss, Wish
Thug love
I shed so many tears
Wishing you were here with me
Life
Wife
I miss your beautiful body. I miss your perfect smell.
I miss the walks in the mall wishing in the wishing well.
Girl, please wait.
Don't leave me.
Girl, please wait!

COMMENTARY

Some boys in detention miss their gangs, which are like family to them. They have fond memories for things they did as a group apart from the violence that resulted in their incarceration. Most students identified with territorial gangs. While the congruence with the gang known as the Skinheads attracts a similar loyalty, sharing a few fundamental characteristics with other gangs, it also has basic differences. The Skinheads are heavily into punk rock, for example, proclaiming it graphically vocalizes their philosophy.

Several punk rock groups enjoy a national audience as well as universal acclaim as an authentic part of the musical world. Skinheads listen to punk music, read stories about the punk groups, and pay rapt attention to the punk message. The tenets of the Skinheads are included in the following essays in an attempt to clarify what my students regarded as general misconceptions.

    A. Information from several discources written on the subject of Skinheads were combined into the following essays. A great deal of time was spent comparing different ideas so all relevant, essential information would be included.
    B. Court staff assigned to my classroom were consulted throughout and acted as sounding boards.

#1 "Prejudice, often thought of as only a black/white thing, is rarely thought to exist between groups within the punk rock scene. Wrong! Skinheads are a huge part of the punk rock scene and the battles of racism rage in many punk rock songs."
#2 "There is the Skinhead who fashions himself a Nazi. There is the Skinhead who calls himself a Sharp (Skinhead Against Racial Prejudice). And, there are a lot of working class Skinheads who believe in neither."
#3 "Skinheads all look much the same: boots with red or white laces, red or white suspenders and, of course, bald heads. They are always mistaken for each other. Where I live there are approximately two thousand organized Nazi Skinheads and about five hundred Sharps. There is also the Unity Punk who'd hope to unite us all together."
#4 "The Nazi Skinheads often call the Sharps and the Unity

Punkers "Two Tones", which means of two colors. It is rank disrespect. The original Skinheads can be traced to Jamaica in the fifties. Black and white, they are considered the traditional Skinheads."

#5 "Today Skinhead boots symbolize the working-class people, and the white laces represent their skin; the red laces represent their blood. Nazi Skinheads are the only ones who are really organized. They own record companies, rent post office boxes, and own compounds in which they are armed with guns. Nazi's have thousands of pieces on the Internet and even have their own magazine. Their leader "TM" is often seen and quoted in the newspaper. He and his father control the major chunk of this organization. It is common knowledge that in California, New York, and the Southern states they are extremely violent."

HISTORICAL PERSPECTIVE

Astonishingly the students knew little about the origins of the Nazi party or Hitler's Germany, unaware of the violence and power of the German state over the people. They were surprised to learn that the Nazi Party was the only German political party in existence at that time. They had no knowledge of the terrorism which reigned in Nazi Germany and how any dissension was silenced vigorously and violently.

They also were unaware that the Nazis opposed <u>all</u> religions or other groups, demanding 100 percent loyalty from their members. Further, they had no understanding of the term "neo-Nazism" or related fascism to the Nazi movement. When told that fascism was taken from the word "fasces," meaning a bundle or union of twigs symbolizing power, they readily agreed that one had to have union in order to have power. Our daily discussions, though brief, proved quite motivational, generating research papers which helped them gain a much more factual grounding and historical perspective on Nazism, and on Nazi Germany and related subjects.

GRAFFITI

Graffiti artisans, called "taggers," describe their passion for graffiti as similar to a person's passion for chocolate, nicotine, or another drug. These "taggers" alluded to feeling a "rush" when engaging in graffiti. The following two narratives are written by "taggers" who devote their lives to much risk-taking in the name of graffiti.

ESSAY #1

"There are two sides to this subject. There is the side taken by the police and homeowners and the side taken by taggers. Most people think that graffiti is either gang writing or just trash on walls.

"The police sometimes put together a sting operation to catch taggers. Undercover cops present themselves as people making a movie about graffiti. They look for gullible taggers who will give them their name, address, and a description of what they write. That description will tell police what crew they are in.

"After the police work this scam for a short time and have enough information on taggers, they go for the arrest. They will round up all the youths who have given them information plus those associated with them.

"People can't believe we would take such risks just to display our works around town. Well, the way taggers feel about graffiti is the way most people feel about chocolate. You do it, you enjoy it, it's a rush worth repeating, that's for sure.

"Graffiti is an art form, a mix of imagination, creativity, and artistic ability. There are many different graffiti groups, some are rivals but most just want to co-exist.

"When it gets down to it, all graffiti writers will pull together when they're harassed. After that sting went down with the phony movie tag, graffiti was everywhere. The tagging crews in town went out and rebelled with a vengeance. We went and "hit up," tagging on the walls--on every wall we could find. Every light pole, white billboard, and train became automatically tagged.

"Some of us had to pay for that and some of us didn't. This should lead us to think deeply about graffiti. When you get down to it graffiti isn't as bad as you think it is. It is an addiction for me and my friends and an object of hate for you people. Remember, rock will never die and neither will graffiti!"

COMMENTARY

The next tagger gives us his historical version of the beginnings of graffiti. He describes its link with skate-boarders, using some of its unique slang as he explains the different types of competition that taggers love. He also reveals the price that parents pay for having a tagger in their household. Finally, he reveals the names of some of the crews that parents may want to keep their children away from.

ESSAY #2

"Graffiti was born in New York back in the late seventies. Affiliated with break dancing and hip hop, graffiti has gained popularity within the last seventeen years throughout the United States. There are many graffiti writers in the world but most of them are in America.

"A lot of skateboarders write Graffiti. It's like a cover-up because the police do not think boarders write. When these skateboarders "click up" together they are called a crew. To get into a crew you have to have artistic skills. Writers will hit up everywhere they can so that they can show off their skills and "click up" with a crew.

"Sometimes crews don't get along and decide to do battle: Where one crew sees another crew's work on the wall and crosses it out and writes over it. These battles can get pretty mean and vicious.

"To avoid violence, taggers have devised another kind of battle where two individual writers go to a wall and see who is better. One tagger will write in his style, and the other person tries to write in a better style. Another way to battle is to see who can "get up" more. That means, whoever is seen more on light poles, bus stops, and walls wins.

"The police are pressured to stop us and they are always trying to trick us. Last year a newspaper asked for graffiti writers for a movie. It turned out to be a sting operation to bust taggers. A lot of people from CIA Crew, UFA Crew, and MD were roped in (The initials of the prominent tagging crews in this community).

"After they went to court most of the kids had to pay fines of up to two thousand dollars. The parents of these kids were hit pretty hard...but that won't stop graffiti!"

COMMENTARY

When gangs write graffiti on walls there's a more sinister message: You'd better respect the territory and stay out if you don't belong! Such writing generates a lot of turf wars which can become extremely vicious. Taggers stay away from that scene as much as possible. They point out that their "art" should not be confused with the scribblings that the gangs engage in throughout our cities.

Federal, state, and local governments have passed very restrictive laws that deal exclusively with drugs. The resultant crackdown and harsher penalties have produced some extreme horror stories. "Thousands of Americans are serving five years in federal prison (with no parole) after being apprehended in possession of less than two pennies' weight of crack--a mere five grams. First offenders who have never even been caught jaywalking automatically receive five years in prison" (Time Out For Justice, Playboy, Dec. 97). Many incarcerated youth feel such laws are an overreaction by government and they make a decent argument for their point of view.

Playboy magazine (same article) reported major abuses of these new laws. The article compared a Rhode Island mass murderer who torched a building killing two adults and four children, and an excavating contractor who was convicted of possession of one-thousand kilos of marijuana. The murderer's sentence makes him eligible for parole in twenty-one years. The contractor charged with drug possession received a twenty-three-year sentence with no possibility of parole.

Another comparison: A man who robbed and killed two brothers in New Orleans, and a computer programmer who grew marijuana in his home for treatment of his arthritis. The murderer plea bargained down to manslaughter, which resulted in an eight-year sentence with parole possible in four years. Because the programmer was a first time drug offender the judge let him off "lightly" with a ninety year sentence!

Such stories have a sobering effect on many of the youngsters who serve time in detention. They know the consequences for drug related crimes can range from a slap-on-the-wrist, to a severe, major, life-altering prison sentence. They know it's a high stakes gamble, but also that there will always be someone--perhaps themselves--who will take that risk.

I asked these youths to describe as best they could the drug related scene happening in their neighborhood. Here are a few of the better essays!

ESSAY #1

"I've sat and watched many friends get ruined by drugs. I've watched them go from high school, college, and good jobs to selling and doing drugs. One was my best friend at the time. He started to put drugs before me and his other friends. This is true of the addict.

"His life went down hill quickly. I tried to help him but me and my friends finally had to disregard him as a friend. We still saw him once in a while and it made us sad to see such a good person go totally rotten.

"Right now he is doing twenty-five to life for cooking "crystal meth." This drug is supposed to make you be more aware and on top of things. No way!

"This drug can be injected, smoked, snorted, or swallowed. To get it you either have to have a lot of money or do what my former friend did. He would go to stores like Lucky, or Vons and steal cold medicines like Efidac Twenty-Four. These medicines contain the drug ephedrine, which is the main ingredient.

"The ephedrine is extracted from the pills, the rest is thrown away. It is then collected and made into powder form. The ephedrine is taken to a person who is called the cooker and is traded for finished crystal meth.

"Three thousand pills will produce one-half ounce of meth. That would be about three hundred boxes of pills. With that amount the cooker can make about seven ounces of meth.

"My friend was called a trader. He got to know the cooker through doing business with him. He then learned to cook and advanced a step higher on the drug ladder. In life he was a step closer to prison or death!

"The cooking process can go on nearly anywhere: a hotel room, apartment, or the house next to you. My friend would move from hotel room to hotel room to elude the cops.

"There are many ways to figure out if this is going on next to you. Look for strange smells, window blinds which never open, and lots of people on the go twenty-four hours a day.

"Once it is cooked the drug can be sold either by the cooker or someone he has sell it for him. I was selling and using this when I was twelve-years-old. Luckily, they locked me up and sent me to a "rehab" camp. It saved me from this problem and I am now "Straight Edge".

"Schools should be aware--when dealers sell they target the high schools. Some of the people I knew only went to school because they wanted to sell. High school students are the main market for crystal meth."

The last writer referred to himself as being "Straight Edge," which is a new movement, a spin-off of the Skinheads. It sounds like something parents would openly welcome. To belong a member must swear off drugs, alcohol, smoking and, astonishingly, even casual sex. Parents, law enforcement, social workers, the community at large should all breathe a sigh of relief and let these "Straight Edge" members enjoy their punk rock concerts as they set an example of clean living for other youth. Not exactly!

Newspaper reporter Arlene Levinson writes a much different

description of the movement operating in Utah. "But, here, the Straight Edge philosophy can also become a bludgeon. Beatings, brawls and vandalism by Straight Edge toughs are common, police say. They say Straight Edgers use chains, mace and clubs to enforce their abstinent lifestyle. Enforcement takes place in school yards, at concerts and shopping center parking lots." (<u>Las Vegas Review Journal/Sun</u>, 12-7-97)

The previous article then quotes Detective Scott Magleby of the Salt Lake City Gang Unit: "If they can't get you, you wake up in the morning, your car will be just pulverized, every window broken out." The article alluded to firebombings and burglaries in the name of rescuing animals. "Straight Edgers have gone further, turning their intolerance on the fur, leather and fast-food trades. Police see the intersection of Straight Edge and the animal rights movement: firebombings of a mink feed cooperative, a McDonald's restaurant, and a Tandy Leather and Crafts Supply store; the near arson of an animal trap business; minks "liberated" from two farms."

Paul, the next writer, talked about moving in and out of numerous using scenes, while meeting people from all walks of life. He scored from, and shot-up with doctors, lawyers, and even police officers. Paul declared it a fact that however people get their money, "by profession or by gun", their real "profession" is feeding their insatiable appetite for drugs. They all pay allegiance to the person holding the drugs, "The Man".

ESSAY #2

"To sell drugs you don't need to have a diploma or a license. You do need to be smart about how you do it, who to sell it to, and who not to sell it to. Selling drugs is like running a lemonade stand. It is there for the people who have to quench their thirst.

"To buy drugs you need to have some kind of job or hustle. I've been able to bum (cadge) sometimes, but I usually ended up robbing people when I was using a lot. My dope dealers had specific, private customers and would not sell to just anybody They would deal with me. I would buy <u>crack</u>, which is priced by the size, and bud, which is sold by the ounce or the way it is sacked. I found that each drug was bought and sold in its special way.

"Using drugs is the only thing that is not hard to do in this business. The rest of it is risky and dangerous. All dealers at some time will come as close to death as possible without actually dying. Many will die! People think using is dangerous. So be it!! As you fight being straight and head back out to score again, you are looking death straight in the eyes!

"There are so many ways to use drugs and so many things to use with them. With weed you can smoke it out of a pipe, roll it in papers, or use a bong. Smoking it is simple. Crack you can almost use the same way and sometimes it is combined with weed and rolled up. I spent most of my time with these two drugs until I was nearly paralyzed by the addiction. My own life and anyone else's had little meaning. Sad, how little the deaths around me bothered me at the time."

COMMENTARY

These stories all have an ominous connection: To live outside the parameters of society is to live in a mean, vicious, and unforgiving place. This is particularly true of gang participation, which is becoming much more lethal. In the fifties, gangs indulged in street fights and occasional knifings. Today they have graduated to using assault rifles and deadly handguns. Murder has become routine business.

Twenty-six youths ages 13 to 19 were slain in Clark County, Nevada in 1996. In her article titled "Young Death", Tanya Flanagan described the devastation an unexpected death caused a family and the pain that will linger for the remainder of their lives (Las Vegas Review Journal, 6-15-97). Twenty-three of the students in the article were identified by my co-workers at juvenile detention as children who had been incarcerated there. The seven pictured in the newspaper looked hauntingly familiar, their smiles misleading. Nine had been enrolled in my GED classes, though none are featured in the essays in this book.

Twenty-four died from gunshot wounds, two were stabbed, the fetus of one victim was killed.

Gang involvement usually <u>starts</u> because the child's family is disorganized and marginally operative. If you are raised in a dysfunctional environment your socialization skills develop outside societal norms and do not serve you well. To fill that void gangs create their own pseudo-family within their unique socialization process which temporarily works better.

Boys and girls who turn to gangs are desperate. They feel useless as individuals because they lack basic necessities such as money or jobs, they are educationally despoiled, and bereft of functional societal skills. In an effort to escape this dire existence they turn to extreme lifestyles. Violence, posturing, and language are used to try to fill the gaping void in their young lives.

The traditional approaches--arrest and incarceration--to dealing with these juvenile problems are limited. We need better and more effective methods. Money must be used for prevention programs if these children are to have any chance for success in the world. Parents, teachers, religious leaders, community leaders, and all concerned adults must work together to begin to create concrete and far-reaching solutions to these problems.

Building more prisons and having children stand trial as adults are not the requisite answers. Authorities and the community must deal decisively and fairly with the youngest of offenders. We must repair our juvenile justice system so that there are consequences for every act of delinquency at the very beginning of the process! Unless we help the child early and offer positive solutions, anything we do later is apt to bear little fruit.

The first crucial step is to train our youth to take responsibility for their own lives. To place blame on one another is futile. We need positive, life affirming actions to turn their lives around. Humans are the only creatures who can make choices about the direction of their lives, then work responsibly to create a peaceful environment rather than one with conflict. Violence, greed, and hatred are the predominate feelings expressed too often by these young people. We must provide opportunities and avenues for change to transform these uncontrolled, untrained minds, and direct them away from the violent impulses which control them.

> "I'm a person just like you
> But I've got better things to do
> Than sit around and smoke dope
> I've got a straight edge."
> (From the song "Straight Edge" by Ian
> MacKaye, the Washington, D.C. based
> band Minor Threat, 1981)

When we deeply analyze all the different aspects of our own human personalities it is apparent that no person is righteously "straight edge." We all have many "edges," some sharp. Children must be taught at an early age that their human flaws can be burnished through training and self-effort, and careful direction. Despite their environment, it need not be a barrier which isolates them from society. We must teach them they are more than their environment, they are individuals in their own right and have the power, with proper guidance, to make healthy, life-affirming choices rather than destructive ones. They can rise above their genes, their heritage, their environment, and gain the wisdom to understand and appreciate the wonderful gift of life and all its wonders.

Chapter 8

THE MISSION: SOLUTIONS
Doing What Needs To Be Done

The teenagers of America have spoken. You have heard their stories and the array of emotions they have openly expressed: from rage to resignation, from defiance to despair, from fear to a deep-seated longing for love. These incarcerated girls and boys, poised on the brink of adulthood, have exhibited flashes of bravada while revealing their vulnerability. These heartbreaking stories of human despair are extraordinary narratives that testify to the lasting, debilitating spell cast on the victims of deeply dysfunctional families. What can we do for these children who are imprisoned in an unresponsive, terrifying home that will give them the will, the courage, the resilience to survive? How can we help them unleash their potential for all that is good and positive?

One BIG question confronts all of us: How can we help these youngsters help themselves? We must make wise and difficult choices in order to implement programs that will provide practical guidelines for tomorrow's adults so they can enjoy the rewards of honest, law-abiding lives. In short, WE MUST PROVIDE THE SOLUTIONS!

*WE = COMMUNITY

Let us first define who "we" are. We are you: parents, teachers, social workers, the community, the judicial system, and law enforcement. Each of these groups must work together in sync and in harmony to keep teens off the streets and out of detention; to keep teens away from gangs and from self-destructive behavior, and to guide them to lead rewarding, productive lives.

Every problem has a solution--either an immediate or ultimate one. Of course, the solution to the problem of teenage violence, rage and criminality is multi-level, multi-dimensional, and complex. To find and implement practical, hands-on solutions demands harmony and concentrated work by all of us-- the parents and the professionals!

In this book, we have given voice to these thoroughly disenfranchised young citizens; now we must give them hope. These incarcerated youth must be offered hope of a meaningful journey. They need to be aware that their life does have meaning, that their painful past will not shape their future, and that we, the community, who will help determine their journey through life, do care.

*Economic Survival

To devise and implement a plan we must start with a solidly plotted solution; a solution imaginatively crafted, solidly textured from facts, and focused in its presentation. Most importantly, we must convince state, county, and city officials that education and social programs are crucial to this country's economic and social survival and advancement. In short, we must prove these programs can pay big dividends. The choice is ours: well equipped schools, stadiums, or convention facilities? Where should the community spend its money? One budget note: Corporate America today states that they believe in helping to finance programs which benefit our youth. Involvement by Corporate America...a definite plus!

Children & Youth Funding Report (CD Publications, 11-4-98) highlighted some corporate sponsors: Bass Hotel and Resorts, which includes Holiday Inn and Crown Plaza Resorts offers grants nationwide for education with no deadlines or amount limits. Citicorp Foundation offers similar grants with a focus on community development and education. Citicorp Foundation supports self-sufficiency for people with mental and physical disabilities, using technology to access educational and job opportunities. Pfizer Inc. awarded $11.7 million in grants, with health care receiving their highest priority. Rite Aid Corporation funds in areas where it has a significant presence and supports programs for families and minorities. The Spencer Foundation supports institutions engaged in research in children and youth issues and selects approximately 200 applications each year for grants of $10,000 or more. Starbucks Foundation, TRW Foundation, and Wal-Mart were also included in the funding report. The funding report, published twice monthly, gives readers tips on how to obtain grants, information on new model programs and innovative fundraising techniques. (Call 1-800-666-6380.)

*A LESSON: MARYLAND VS. VIRGINIA

In Maryland, the city of Baltimore opted to spend $500 million on their sports facilities, Camden Yards and Ravens Stadium, hoping to create a bonanza of new jobs as well as enhancing the tax base. Conversely, Virginia focused their economic development strategy on their education system, from kindergarten through college. In Kiplinger's list of the top 25 public universities five are in Virginia. In contrast, Maryland has only one of its public universities on the list. In fact, Virginia's top-of-the-line educational system has spawned a spectacular boom in full-time, non-seasonal and high wage jobs connected to high-tech industry. In contrast, Baltimore's middle-class population fled to the suburbs and their building program, Camden Yards and Ravens Stadium, produced a paltry number of low-paying jobs.

Ronald D. Utt, a Fellow in Budgetary Affairs at Heritage Foundation writes: Virginia's "emphasis on education gives it a competitive edge in attracting jobs and job-seekers. Professor Robert Baade of Lake Forest College in Illinois found that of 30 cities that built stadiums between 1958 and 1989, 27 showed no change in per-capita income, and three experienced significant declines." (Las Vegas Review Journal, 10-12-98)

Clearly, the information above indicates education is a key factor in a city's overall economic success, one of many factors crucial to solving the teen crime problem. A dynamic, powerful, hard-hitting organization is needed to produce results similar to those in Virginia. Teachers in Politics (TIP) is a good example of what individuals can do to make their profession a highly visible group that is forcefully heard in the political arena. When

I became the first chairman of Teachers in Politics (TIP) in Nevada in 1970 it became immediately apparent that if we expected to be successful we had to be highly organized and visible to the community at large, as well as the elected officials specifically. Fortunately, former state senator and attorney John Foley, a member of a prominent, well-respected political family had worked in politics with his father, Judge Foley, for many years and offered the model for TIP. An old army buddy of mine, he graciously offered his law offices in the evenings as a gathering place for teachers, meticulously outlining the fundamentals for such an organization.

First we had to deal with hundreds of frustrated teachers in the county who felt helpless, manipulated, and powerless when confronted with the dual demands of teaching and rearing their own families. In order to tap the creative imagination of this smoldering, as yet unresponsive political body, John Foley explained the fundamental (and ultimately) most important action we had to take. TIP created a card file with the address and phone number of each teacher, noting what each would be willing to do in an election year. This involved chairing a candidate's campaign, walking their own and/or other precincts, displaying a yard sign or bumper sticker, hosting a tea for their candidate, assembling yard and street signs, using their garage for an area campaign headquarters, etc. We also established media contacts to explain our efforts, publicize our message, and generate positive publicity for our teachers. After I persuaded five of my best friends to help with TIP, we discussed in depth how we could begin with maximum efficiency. We all agreed that the local teachers association would be the logical organization to work with. The receptive leadership appointed me chairman and my friends the committee members of TIP. Motivated and energized for action we enjoyed unprecedented success. We elected nearly 80 percent of our endorsed ticket and, more importantly, we were becoming the model for teacher organizations throughout the country.

*TRANSCEND POLITICS

Admittedly, it's often easier to motivate professional groups to take action, but what about the concerned mother, father, grandparent, or ordinary citizen who want to become involved? Although the work is the same there needs to be a like-minded organization to welcome the ideas of these individuals. There are dozens of service and social groups in virtually all U.S. communities. The first step is to initiate contact and become involved. Determine what the focus of the group is in terms of education and teen crime, then work with them to devise and initiate a specific plan of action.

*FAMILIES IN CRISIS: WHAT IS WORKING!

Throughout this book we have read the brash, emotional, angry stories of today's incarcerated youths which have revealed the primeval nature of teen life in much of America. Now we must dissect their thoughts and draw some practical conclusions. We need to unearth the best solutions to these overwhelming problems in our turbulent and troubled cities. Let's first see what does work.

Across the USA, states are increasingly taking immediate steps to remove children from unhealthy homes and end parental rights if the environment is deemed potentially dangerous to the physical and mental well-being of the child. Lawmakers are, in fact, getting tough on welfare agencies, parents, and judges. With the increased need for social services, the government persistently seeks ways to cut costs while at the same time adding needed services. Functions formerly run by the public sector are now being privatized. Marcon/Choices Unlimited, where I work as a consultant, is an example of a private company which works cooperatively with the courts, addressing the drug problems of both juveniles and adults. Founded by a former co-worker of mine at juvenile detention, it provides important counseling, educational and employment consultation, drug testing, and acupuncture to both juvenile and adult drug offenders. Working directly with the Eighth Judicial Court, this program has eliminated incarceration for a sizable population and at the same time saved valuable funds for other uses.

Throughout America private companies such as Marcon/Choices Unlimited are assuming tasks formerly thought of as strictly public sector endeavors. They are running youth prisons, managing group homes for children unable to live at home because of delinquent behavior, addiction problems or other difficulties. Many children who are unable to function in conventional schools because of mental illnesses or other diagnosed problems are being treated in private institutions.

The cost of dealing with these dysfunctional family situations often engenders resistance from a wide spectrum of special-interest groups in the local communities. Many want to opt for the cheapest solution, but not necessarily the best. These groups must be educated and constantly reminded that it is fiscally sound to deal with these problems quickly, decisively, and prudently. Delays drastically increase the financial burden to <u>all</u> constituents.

*GRANTS-BIG BUSINESS

Private industry recognizes that juvenile justice programs offer a lucrative market for their investment funds; thus they are increasingly entering into partnership programs with the local public entities. The DCA (Drug-Free Communities Act 1997) is releasing considerable funding for grant applicants (public and private). President Clinton announced in September 1998 that 93 grants totaling 8.7 million was being released. "As part of the FY '99 budget deal Congress doubled the DCA appropriation to $20 million, which should yield another 100 grantees." (<u>Youth Today</u>, Vol 8, No.1, December/ January 1999) The newspaper also pointed out that this is just a trickle compared to the $17.1 billion in annual federal monies allocated for the war on drugs.

The number of juveniles in these programs is expected to double by the year 2005, growing faster than the juvenile population as a whole (<u>The Miami Herald,</u> 11-29-98)." Currently there are over 10,000 independent providers of these services across the U.S.A. Excellent opportunities exist for well-trained professionals to become independent operatives, working without the cumbersome layers of bureaucracy that often stifle creativity.

Focusing on the inhospitable family environment and implementing important programs for at-risk and troubled youth requires three things, initially costly on face value, but cost effective in the long term. They are:

1] Increase the number of caseworkers significantly
2] Enhance funding to the state agency handling services to children
3] Most importantly, exercise diligence and imagination in <u>securing permanent homes</u> for these youngsters

How can one person significantly aid in accomplishing this? Primarily through the political system. "If you look back 10 years, you saw almost every single political race was being run on a platform of health care reform. Now almost every single political platform includes education and children's safety and crime prevention." (<u>Miami Herald</u>, ll-29-98) The "business" of taking care of our youth is crucial to a state or city's economic survival. Businessmen and politicians are now more aware of this fact than ever before. Like-minded community members must mobilize, uniting in this critical cause: the basic survival and emotional well-being of our youth. Their overall nurturing must be the focus of all efforts to help today's troubled teens.

*TEEN PREGNANCY-SPECIFIC PROGRAMS

WE CAN, INC., a national and state-by-state organization for the prevention of child abuse, is also focusing on the widespread problem of teen pregnancy, and they seek help in this uphill battle.

Often these young mothers are incapable of providing the warm, caring family setting that is so crucial for children in their formative years. The average income for female-headed families in 1988 was $16,000, compared with married couples with

$37,000 per year. (U.S. Census Bureau, 1990) This clearly does not give the child being reared in a female-headed household a level field when they start life. Here, professionals and business groups alike must influence school curriculum to ensure that teens are exposed to positive influences that could help negate teen pregnancy. Politically, we need to begin with the elected Board of Education. The Board makes the final decisions on how money is spent, what programs are emphasized, and whether all schools are treated equally in the distribution of funds. Each school has its own special requirements. In my experience, the local Board is the easiest, most receptive place for the initiation of political activism in the community at large.

*CHILDREN AT RISK PROJECT/CHARTER SCHOOLS

Operating in six cities across America, The Children at Risk Project currently provides intensive interventions for selected poor children in six cities. This project is funded at just $4,000 per child. Compare this figure with the incarceration cost per child which exceeds $20,000. The consequences of child poverty are estimated in the billions--approximately 36 billion in 1995 alone. These figures alone make a strong case for local officials to adopt the at-risk concept. Everything revolves around education, social class, family structure and, ultimately, for these children, societal intervention.

Throughout the nation there are over 1,200 government-funded charter schools, many designed to specifically meet the needs of children with special requirements. Most are run by private groups. Hopefully, the success or failure of these endeavors are being carefully monitored so that we can learn from this growing part of the educational system. Another 800 are expected to open by September and some of these will provide help for children with special education needs. Unequivocably, there is growing concern among such professional groups as the National Education Association (NEA) about charter schools and their role in the larger educational scheme. Obviously there will be careful scrutiny by professional organizations who feel threatened by these private groups. But a cautious mix of the two is a plausible approach to seeking new solutions.

*GANGS: MEETING THE CHALLENGE

Nationally, gangs are a burgeoning subculture with roots reaching into all economic/social levels of their respective communities. According to James C. Howell of the <u>U.S. Department of Justice</u>, "Police and FBI officials have asserted that the Los Angeles Bloods and Crips have migrated to 45 other cities and set up drug trafficking operations. Most of the drug trafficking in the two cities these officials believe to be major gang migration cities, Kansas City and Seattle, has also been attributed to the Crips and Bloods gangs. Klein and Maxson's studies show gang migration into 713 of over 1100 cities studied. The youth gang problem is also increasing from the standpoint of more violent offenses, more serious injuries, and more lethal weapons." (Office of Juvenile Justice and Delinquency Prevention, 4-15-94)

Youth gangs account for a sizable and growing percentage of all homicides as they infiltrate all the pathways of criminal activity from violence and drug trafficking, to the disruption of the public educational system. On the home front, what can parents themselves do to keep their offspring away from the toxic influence of gang activity?

The sad fact is we are becoming a nation living in fear of our own children. The parental unit itself is in dire need of immediate attention. Why would a child shun a home to become a gang member whose life is described as nasty, brutish, and short lived? Obviously the home fails to offer the security, comfort, and love of a stable family. When we successfully offer these families the help they need we will make great strides in stopping the bloody rampage of gangs loose on the streets!

*ACTIVE SOLUTIONS:

We must support our law enforcement in cracking down swiftly and resolutely on gang participation. For example, Los

Angeles has had success with its ban on <u>any</u> public gang association in target areas throughout the city. Court orders ban standing, sitting, walking, driving or appearing anywhere in the target area with a known gang member. Police confiscate drugs, paraphernalia, beepers, cellular phones, police scanners, and weapons. The message is that all available tools will be used to curb illegal gang activity.

The community must be involved in the process. If your community has not implemented this type of decisive action, make your voice heard. Go to your local planning board. Consider volunteering in some capacity. If you live in Los Angeles and you feel they are not enforcing these objectives <u>make your voice heard!</u> Work within your community to organize a liaison group to work cooperatively with law enforcement!

Additional action includes: Initiating a "Letters to the Editor Campaign" involving friends, neighbors, and parents. Newspapers spur other members of the community to action. Surveys indicate the "Letters to the Editor" section is one of the most widely read sections of the newspaper and a highly effective way to disperse ideas and initiate action. Also, involve your local politicians-- Mayor, D.A., Representative.

*MENTOR PROGRAM

Mentoring is progressively recognized nationally as a remarkable and effective way to positively influence youth, especially the disadvantaged. To take children "under wing" helps them to avoid the pitfalls of gang criminality. For example, the Youth Aid Panel in Philadelphia produced some interesting statistics: Youngsters in their mentoring program were nearly 50 percent <u>less</u> likely to initiate drug use, about 25 percent less likely to use alcohol, and a third less likely to commit an assault!

A successful real estate broker in Los Angeles is a mentor to a black youth from a drug-addicted family. The boy is learning computer skills as well as social skills. His progress, notes his mentor, "has been remarkable." Claire McCarthy, M.D. and author of Everyone's Children, decided her career as a pediatrician would make a bigger difference at an inner-city health clinic that serves some of the poorest families in Boston. She describes what many in the medical profession consider unthinkable; becoming personally involved in the lives of her patients. From helping them receive appropriate legal services to opening her home for a night, she has been more than their medical doctor...she's a fated mentor in their lives.

"We are not meant to parent alone. We are meant to be part of a community, where hands come out to guide us and help hold our children, where voices chime and mingle with ours, teaching us, comforting us. Our children are meant to grow up under many watchful eyes, and to have the love and encouragement of many." (Claire McCarthy, M.D., Family Resource Coalition of America Report, Summer/Fall 1998, Vol. 17, Nos. 2-3)

The mentoring factor is extremely effective when dealing with youth whose gang affiliation has a low level of group cohesion. It distinctly lowers the number and extent of serious crime. The Partnership for a Drug Free America's web site (www.drugfreeamerica. org.) offers help to families trying to combat the problems of drug abuse and also helps to reduce other risks to their children. "The success of the Partnership so far has been the result of the combined efforts of parents, schools, and all members of the community." (Ibid.) The Partnership is funded by the Robert Wood Johnson Foundation and more than 200 private sector corporations. They are also the primary adviser to the White House national anti-drug media campaign.

*CHURCH MENTORS

The church is a uniquely visible institution in the battle against youth-oriented crime. The Church offers wonderful mentoring opportunities. If your church is not active in mentoring take steps to urge it in this direction. Church volunteers who mentor "front-end" juvenile offenders have proven to be very effective.

Professionals in the juvenile field discovered long ago that working with such community volunteers has a profound, positive effect on young people.

The 7.1 million children growing up in poor communities, (<u>Kids Count, 1997</u>, The Annie E. Casey Foundation) are at greater risk of not having adequate health care, getting pregnant or fathering a child, using drugs, exposure to violence, and of being jailed before they reach adulthood. These children deserve a better chance, and the one place that chance survives and often flourishes, is the church. If we can encourage and nurture this valuable community asset these children have a chance to escape these grim statistics. Fellowship, the personal counseling, and other wonderful activities offered by the church that many of us experienced growing up, proved to be valuable factors in creating and nurturing positive behavior and attitudes in all of us.

*GENERATION TO GENERATION

Unemployment, school failure, child abuse, gang participation, teen pregnancy, and prostitution are toxic elements in our communities. We must all work together to eliminate these negative factors. We need a <u>fresh</u> exploration of these eternal questions: Where am I from? Where do I belong? Where do I go from here? What meaning does my life have? Can I realize my potential? Most importantly: Can I reinvent the tale?

For generations we have observed the following basic facts. These children are:

1] prone to emotional problems
2] often end up in juvenile court
3] are far more apt to repeat negative behavior and in the process often become abusive parents--WE CAN, INC. released statistics which indicated that 90 percent of juvenile and adult prisoners claim abuse as children.

*UNEMPLOYMENT

The staggering rate of unemployment in crime-immersed communities such as Los Angeles is targeted as the most significant factor in the epidemic of violence. "The absence of jobs in the conventional economy is widely viewed as responsible for pushing young persons into drug dealing; economic incentives have been suggested as a means of coopting gang members." (Daniel J. Monti, GANGS, State University of New York Press, Albany, 1993)

Many families repeat patterns of unemployment through the third or fourth generations! From this perspective, the future looks bleak. Look closely at unemployment and its devastating contribution to the epidemic of crime. According to the Los Angeles Police Department Census Bureau (1997) the most significant factor identified in gang-related homicides is unemployment and per capita income. Without gainful employment an already delinquent teen is attracted to a gang thus becoming more violently delinquent in the gang. As the education/work consultant for Marcon I know first-hand how difficult it is to place a youngster in the job market if he or she has the visible look of a gang member. The things they prize most, their hair, clothes, body markings, and even mannerisms, are the things they must change if they are to be welcomed by the businessman in today's market.

*UNDERLYING FORCES

In order to fully implement programs successfully, we must also understand the historical and social forces which mold teenagers today. Frederic Thrasher's benchmark study of 1,313 Chicago gangs, first published in 1927, astonishingly describes the attitudes and motivation of the typical gang member today. Only the cast of characters has changed: he described Euro-immigrant teens, mostly Caucasian, while today gang members embody more ethnic and racial diversity. Sadly, the lack of an appropriate model/mentor to guide them in their struggle to successfully adjust to society is still imperious in their gang-dominated lives. They must be enlightened, helped to recognize the fundamentally negative disposition of gang society which shatters their hope for a better life.

In the 1920's Thrasher wrote about Chicago's adolescent gang activities which consisted mostly of stealing and vandalism.

Appalled by their behavior, he said they had "no moral opprobrium" for these activities. Compare that with today's youthful gangsters who sells illegal drugs with similar moral abandon. Armed with semi-automatic military weapons, today's teens are a <u>far</u> greater danger to themselves and others. Today's social outcast is more dangerous to society because, while psychology changes little, the social/cultural climate has become more violent.

*SCHOOLS/CURRICULUM REFORM

To give youth a meaningful modicum of hope, schools must redesign high school curriculum to meet the needs of youngsters who require basic instruction, unlike other students who are ready to prepare for college. One of the best approaches to curriculum reform could be modeled on the GED/basic education mode. This prepares students in the basic subjects of math, English, writing, and history, giving them the fundamental tools for the job market. This requires mostly a change in approach rather than a huge infusion of funds. This attainable goal could be accomplished with an enlightened school board plus community-involved teachers, school administrators, social workers, and concerned citizens. Again, a concerted harmony among all relevant groups.

*DRUGS AND ADDICTION

During the nineties drug-related crimes have more than doubled and continue to grow. FBI released statistics reveal that arrests jumped from 64,000 in 1990 to 147,000 by 1995 (L.A.Times, 12-26-96).

An alarming 80 percent of jailed detainees stated they used

either drugs or alcohol during their criminal activities. Most authorities consider alcohol as somehow less dangerous than "hard drugs". But The National Center on Addiction and Substance Abuse indicates that alcohol plays a larger role in violent crime than either crack or powder cocaine. What further complicates this disturbing picture is today's teens fascination with guns and the expanding drug scene. The availability of guns and other deadly weapons must be stopped--by laws and by parental/community involvement. The profitable drug trafficking helps finance other criminal activities. Greed and power fight an unending battle for the cherished spoils that drugs spew on an individual, their neighborhood and community. Underlying many of our basic problems in the juvenile sector is the overwhelming growth in illicit drug use and the proliferation of drug sales in the schools themselves.

My involvement with the Eighth Judicial Court's effort to deal with illicit teenage drug use has heightened my awareness of the acute need for cooperation among all entities. This cooperative effort must include the court, juvenile probation, the schools, local businesses, and the family, plus counseling, drug screening, and other therapeutic care. In my role as school/job coordinator I interrelate with all segments of this network. It is significant to note that when these groups function as one cooperative unit, success is likely. Conversely, a breakdown in any area would certainly spell failure.

Increasingly, parents are viewed as being <u>responsible</u> for overseeing their child's behavior. This creates some valid concerns for parents. A good example is the liability factor for those who favor guns in the house. This "responsibility" theme is being repeated by the court, probation, school, the employer, the social agency, and others affiliated with the family unit. As they put their shattered body and spirit-- literally their life--back together it is absolutely necessary that the parent assume a responsible and responsive role. It is becoming increasingly obvious to an enlightened citizenry that only a solid, united effort will make a dent in this in-your-face menace as it affects all levels of society.

"More than 90 percent of the arrestees tested at the

Henderson and Clark County Detention Center were taken into custody under the influence of alcohol, and almost 70 percent were under the influence of some kind of drug, preliminary findings of a new study show." (<u>Las Vegas Sun</u>, 12-24-98) This Las Vegas, Nevada study is part of the National Institute of Justice study started in 1987, one of 35 cities involved in feeding information to their Washington D.C. office. Marijuana was the most common illegal drug found in the tests, along with cocaine, methamphetamine, and opiates. Four out of every ten detainees arrested for violent crimes tested positive for drugs! Never underestimate the enormous cost of drugs in our society! Hopefully this significant study will encourage a comprehensive review of the complexities and impact of issues as they surface throughout the U.S.A.

*PIMPS, PROSTITUTION, THE LAW

The American Correctional Association in 1994 stated that sexually abused girls are at greater risk than other runaways. Abused girls will escape at any cost, often under the worst conditions. One can only imagine how extremely painful home must be if they are willing to exchange that for the precarious and dangerous life on the road.

Disturbing stories on prostitution illustrate a bewildering relationship between the pimp and the youngster he drives around the country, who wantonly risks her life to disease or physical mayhem. Prostitution both sustains and suffocates the girls involved. These females must perform a complicated balancing act to satisfy the greed of their pimp while attracting clientele and avoiding the law.

We must pressure our state legislators to enact laws which deal swiftly and punitively with the pimps who exploit these girls. They are little more than slaves to the pimp. <u>L.A.Times</u> staff writer Davan Maharaj (12-27-95) described a "slave bracelet" that a pimp gave a young prostitute to signify that she was his <u>property</u>!

"Eugene, Oregon Police Department detective Greg Harvey said he was shocked to find during an investigation that pimps in his state arrange for false identification for girls and order them to find jobs in Nevada brothels. The girls then send earnings to the pimps, Harvey contends." (Las Vegas Review Journal, 1-21-98) Through Harvey's efforts one pimp was convicted of 31 counts of coercion. (He is developing cases against other Oregon pimps.) This type of dogged pursuit is the best answer to reign in the pimp who preys on runaway and homeless youth.

When the Mary Magdalene Project recently opened its 12 unit apartment in Van Nuys California (L.A.Times, 12-2-96) it was noted that this organization was one of the very few in the entire nation which assists prostitutes. The article revealed the lack of fundamental education, work, or social skills these young females have when they start the rehabilitation process. Many cannot even tell time or use a simple calendar. The Project helps them learn skills for daily living, while providing a refuge from the streets.

Right now, most laws deal more harshly with drug offenders than with pimps. Professionals in the work force must constantly be alert to young girls who are in danger of falling into this syndrome. We must make certain that all community resources are available to her and her family. A fresh perspective is needed on this entire problem prevalent in all American cities, large and small. We cannot continue to treat prostitution as a criminal problem while we ignore the social aspects that trap them into such a hopeless, dead-end situation. There are many social ramifications to this problem that must be recognized and dealt with on many levels.

*CHILD ABUSE

Child abuse and neglect is the most detectable and visible cause of teenage prostitution. But it may incubate for years, undetectable except for occasional early warnings. Abuse is toxic to the minds of the victims until they finally collapse under the strain and are forced to heedlessly engage in self-destructive behavior. Active programs must be implemented to stop this blight on society now!

One solution: Every member of the community must be alert to any signs of child abuse and report any suspicions immediately. In l996 alone close to <u>one</u> <u>million</u> cases of child abuse were confirmed via reports from teachers, police, doctors, family members, friends, and neighbors. These groups and individuals must be trained, educated, or otherwise prepared to be alert to <u>early</u> <u>signs</u> of possible abuse.

Children who are left unsupervised, particularly by parents who may have alcohol or drug problems, are likely targets. Anyone noticing such a situation must call protective services and report this. Far beyond this, however, our greater task is to ignite a <u>National</u> <u>Awareness</u> <u>Program</u> about child safety and the risks children face in abusive, dysfunctional and dangerous homes.

Physical or sexual abuse often requires the removal of an abusive, violent parent or other adult from the home. Unfortunately, this is not as simple as it sounds. Incredibly, many states require changes in their laws before this can be accomplished. The bedrock principle behind protective services in most states is to reunite the child with their families and this pervades the thinking of local legislators. But laws must be changed to allow for the separation of child from the family if it is in the <u>best</u> <u>interest</u> <u>of</u> <u>the</u> <u>child</u>. We must get abused and neglected children out of these abusive homes as quickly as possible! Futher, if the assessment for reuniting the parent with the child is poor this should be permanent. "The most difficult families to reach are resistant families who have failed to integrate the social, emotional, and cognitive competencies needed for healthy child and human development. Parents in resistant families often exhibit serious functional problems such as extreme disorganization, substance abuse, poor conception of boundaries, deficient parenting skills, and exposure to and experience with extreme violent behavior. These families have traditionally been the poorest candidates for prevention and have not responded well to treatment services." (Daro and Gelles, <u>Journal of Interpersonal Violence</u>, Sage Periodicals Press, 12-92) The article stated that few of these families responded to public awareness and education campaigns, which bolsters the argument that these children absolutely have to be removed from these homes.

Each individual state must re-examine their current laws. Removal of a potentially dangerous parent or other adult in the home may be crucial to saving a child's life. Lacking a central national core, we must rely on the wisdom of each state legislature to enact the laws that directly protect the child from their immediate environment. But this dark, secret world must be exposed to the light so that positive steps can be taken toward rebuilding the lives of these victims.

*SURVIVAL CONCLUSIONS

The problems of teen crime and violence are extremely complex and each requires intense and ongoing efforts on the part of all concerned citizens. Nothing can be accomplished if we flee into our individual havens, hoping the conflict will resolve itself. Instead, we must carefully examine what is wrong and what is right with the present system. The kinds of transitions which we hope to accomplish will not be done in a month or a year; they will require ongoing and focused teamwork and dedication by all members of the larger community. All of us must become part of that larger community, part of a dedicated team working toward common goals. Changes always produce stress and when that occurs many shrink from the task. But we must turn this stress into creative and productive modes so that we can reinvent the system in a healthy, positive manner. There will be broad variations in the tasks we assume and the gut-wrenching level at which we work to implement these evolving changes in our society. We must be equal to the task!

One thing is certain, we must strive for new solutions. Specialists in the many fields will have to work together to cross-fertilize their findings. If we work diligently there will still be major setbacks and we will have to find ways to adapt. The methodology is out there if we are willing to search and work very diligently to rewrite the script. We must work to change that which must be changed. In 1884 Olive Schreiner wrote: "The barb in the arrow of childhood suffering is this: its intense loneliness, its intense ignorance." (The Story of an African Farm,

1884) Although voiced over one hundred years ago this observation is still vividly poignant today!

In his 1937 Inaugural Address President Franklin Delano Roosevelt stated; "The test of progress is not whether we add more to the abundance of those who have much; it is whether we provide enough for those who have too little." That is the challenge of all concerned adults today! We must focus intensely on solutions now.

> What have you done, you there,
> Weeping incessantly,
> Tell me, what have you done
> With your youth?
> Paul Verlaine, Sagesse, 1881

A P P E N D I X

Here, listed in no particular order, are awards and letters of commendation which were alluded to in parts of the book.

1. State of Nevada--A PROCLAMATION--By the Governor

2. Honorary Life Membership--Nevada Parent/Teacher Association

3. Letter of commendation--Clark County School District Superintendent, Dr. Robert E. Wentz

4. Letter of commendation--Clark County Juvenile Court Services Director, Robert J. Ranney

5. Participant--Surrogate Parent Program

6. Distinguished Service Award--Clark County School District Nevada